The Tort of Discovery Abuse

Recent Titles from Quorum Books

Private Pensions and Employee Mobility: A Comprehensive Approach to Pension Policy
Izzet Sahin

Group Decision Support Systems for Effective Decision Making: A Guide for MIS Practitioners and End Users
Robert J. Thierauf

Deregulation and Competition in the Insurance Industry
Banks McDowell

Chemical Contamination and Its Victims: Medical Remedies, Legal Redress, and Public Policy
David W. Schnare and Martin T. Katzman, editors

Statistics for Real Estate Professionals
Rebecca F. Guy and Louis G. Pol

Decision-Aiding Software and Legal Decision-Making: A Guide to Skills and Applications Throughout the Law
Stuart S. Nagel

Regulatory Interventionism in the Utility Industry: Fairness, Efficiency, and the Pursuit of Energy Conservation
Barbara R. Barkovich

The Acceptance of Human Resource Innovation: Lessons for Management
Ellen Ernst Kossek

Doing Away with Personal Injury Law: New Compensation Mechanisms for Victims, Consumers, and Business
Stephen D. Sugarman

International Transfer Pricing Policies: Decision-Making Guidelines for Multinational Companies
Wagdy M. Abdallah

The Privilege to Keep and Bear Arms: The Second Amendment and Its Interpretation
Warren Freedman

The Tort of Discovery Abuse

WARREN FREEDMAN

Q
QUORUM BOOKS
New York • Westport, Connecticut • London

Library of Congress Cataloging-in-Publication Data

Freedman, Warren.
The tort of discovery abuse.

Bibliography: p.
Includes index.
1. Discovery abuse—United States. I. Title.
II. Title: Discovery abuse.
KF1270.5.F74 1989 347.73'72 88-32441
347.30772
ISBN 0-89930-332-3 (lib. bdg. : alk. paper)

British Library Cataloguing in Publication Data is available.

Library of Congress Catalog Card Number: 88-32441
ISBN: 0-89930-332-3

First published in 1989 by Quorum Books

Greenwood Press, Inc.
88 Post Road West, Westport, Connecticut 06881

Printed in the United States of America

The paper used in this book complies with the Permanent Paper Standard issued by the National Information Standards Organization (Z39.48-1984).

10 9 8 7 6 5 4 3 2 1

Contents

Preface

Familiarity with the discovery process is vital to an understanding of abuses of the discovery process. Part I delineates what discovery is all about; it is comparable to the mixing of ingredients and the baking of the birthday cake. Part II, on the other hand, is not only the lighting of the candles but the consumption and enjoyment of the cake.

In short, the author seeks to establish a modern-day "tort of discovery abuse," a cause of action that exists independently of whatever sanctions a court may impose for discovery abuse. But to reach that stage in Part II, the first 10 chapters must deal with the discovery process in action. The author's 1987 book *Frivolous Lawsuits and Frivolous Defenses* (Quorum Books) utilized a mere four pages on discovery abuses as an example of unjustifiable litigation; but the focus in Part II takes a more pragmatic view than simply that of "unjustifiable litigation." Here the author examines the new tort of discovery abuse, including spoliation or destruction of evidence, overindulgence in freedom of information, and a detailed analysis of sanctions ordered by courts. Chapter 16 sets forth the intentional tort of discovery abuse in all its ramifications.

In summary, Part I explicates the nature of the discovery process and logically and chronologically precedes Part II on the nature of the abuses of the discovery process.

PART I

THE NATURE OF THE DISCOVERY PROCESS

1

Introduction to the Discovery Process

Discovery, the objective of which is to ascertain the information in the possession of the opposing party in litigation, has been sociologically delineated in terms of "manifest" and "latent" functions.[1] While the manifest purpose of discovery is to discover all relevant information, it is said that the latent purpose of discovery is to exhaust the opponent both economically and psychologically. Admittedly, this distinction may have few scholastic or academic supporters; but, in truth, the search for information in advance of trial has been plagued by the high costs necessitated by compliance with discovery authorizations. Indeed, it may be pointed out that the cost of pursuing a case to trial by indulging in the discovery process can embarrass (and even cause default by) the economically weaker party to the litigation. Psychologically, a party to the litigation can be subject to painful and humiliating questions in the discovery process, especially since the scope of permissible discovery under the liberal federal rules is extremely wide, and more states have adopted these federal rules on discovery than any other set of federal provisions on procedure.[2] The search for truth is thus given a big boost.

It is said that discovery, especially pretrial discovery, has become the center of gravity in modern litigation.[3] The thrust is simply that one party during the discovery process attempts to prove its case to the other party so as to induce settlement on favorable terms. The winning strategy is to obtain all necessary information at the minimum cost of time and money, unless the avowed purpose of the discovery is the latent and almost cynical function described above.[4]

The liberalized rules on discovery in both state and federal courts means that the parties to the litigation will each utilize all available means to discover facts that might in some way or manner be relevant to the litigation-inducing event.[5] The objectives of discovery, while differing in criminal as opposed to civil cases, are essentially clear: obtain evidence not later obtainable at time of trial; formulate, isolate, and narrow the issues for trial; and develop leads to the existence of additional evidence that would be admissible at trial.

In the federal courts, Rule 26(b) of the Federal Rules of Civil Procedure defines the scope of discovery as ''any matter not privileged, which is relevant to the subjectmatter involved in the pending action.'' Subparagraph (1) includes any matter not privileged that is ''reasonably calculated to lead to the discovery of admissible evidence.'' Federal Rules 26 to 37 on discovery practice permit the use of interrogatories addressed to the parties, requests for production of documents or things or permission to enter property, depositions taken from both written and oral questions, requests for admission of fact, and requests for physical and mental examinations.[6] A brief look at each of these ''tools'' of discovery is in order.

Interrogatories, unfortunately, are often inadequate when directed at large institutions to obtain complex and technical data because of the number of information gatherers and the unavailability of the precise information requested; interrogatories are a more useful discovery device when dealing with smaller organizations.[7]

Requests for documents must be comprehensive, at least in contrast to interrogatories, which have a limited deployment in ordinary tort actions; one of the pragmatic problems is business management's penchant for destruction of documents as part of a ''records retention'' program. Another defeating technique that can frustrate requests for documents is a company's use of independent custodians of documents so that the company can straightforwardly state that it does not have custody of the documents.[8]

Depositions are probably the most common tools of discovery because in face-to-face confrontation the truth may generally be obtained, although the expensiveness of a full set of depositions might militate against their use.

Requests for admissions is an especially powerful tool for litigation of complex scientific and technical issues; resort to the court for clarification of answers may become necessary, but the time and effort so expended is rewarding. Simple demands that the deposee admit to the authenticity of a document, for example, or to the learned treatise status of the source from which the expert facts are drawn, will readily result (if the deposee does not so admit, a motion limited to compelling such admission can be made).

Affidavits are perhaps one of the neglected tools of discovery; affidavits can be fruitfully used to address virtually any issue or problem, whether it be to obtain an attachment or to prove prior notice of the claim; affidavits can establish simple facts material to the litigation.

The myriad issues surrounding the discovery process can perhaps be illustrated by several cases set forth herein, to wit:

1. *Cipollone v. Liggett Group, Inc.*, where the Third U.S. Court of Appeals authorized the sharing of discovery materials among lawyers with similar cases against the same defendant, contrary to the obvious wishes of the defendant cigarette company.[9] Subsequent claimants need not expend the time and money to obtain the same discovery materials, and thus the entire discovery process is more readily opened up.[10]

2. *New York Yankees Partnership v. Sportschannel Associates,*[11] where a broad protective order against disclosure by the New York Yankees of allegedly sensitive trade secrets was denied because public policy was in favor of full disclosure,[12] thus exposing truth in a public interest situation.

3. *Boehm v. E. F. Hutton & Co.*, where the federal court appeared sensitive to confidentiality issues and granted defendant's request for a protective order against production of certain documents because the court found that the defendant (who sought protection) had made a sufficient showing that "it might suffer serious harm in its highly competitive investment bank business if documents requested by plaintiff fell into the hands of its competitors."[13]

4. An attorney who flouted a court order that he produce a certain witness in a federal district court trial in San Diego, California, found that, as a result, the court had entered a default and dismissed his client's action, which meant that his client would have to pay damages of more than $100 million unless the order was reversed on appeal.[14] According to the court, "a total refusal to cooperate with opposing counsel, playing games, tactical or otherwise, with court and counsel"

merited the summary ruling of sanctions, not against the offending counsel but against his client.

5. *Frank v. Capital Cities Communications, Inc.*,[15] where the federal district court resolved two timely discovery issues, namely, the circumstances under which one party may take the deposition of its adversary's attorney and whether counsel has an absolute right to obtain copies of confidential documents produced for inspection by an adversary.[16]

The discovery process is always dependent upon "relevancy" of the information requested, i.e., the information sought must be relevant to the subject matter involved in the pending action. But relevant, nonadmissible evidence is discoverable if it will lead to admissible evidence. The identity and whereabouts of any witness who is thought to have discoverable information is one example of relevant, nonadmissible testimonial evidence.[17] Privileged matter, however, is not discoverable, but the privilege must be asserted by the person who could assert the privilege at trial.[18] There is also "immunity" from discovery of materials prepared by counsel for trial purposes as well as immunity from discovery of opinions of experts that counsel has consulted in trial preparation.[19]

Discovery is "reciprocal" under Rule 16 of the Federal Rules of Criminal Procedure, i.e., if a defendant requests and receives disclosure of documents, tangible objects, or government scientific reports, the government or prosecution may request and receive access to similar materials in the possession of the defendant.[20] But the defendant must have, in fact, requested and received discovery,[21] and the prosecution's request must have been reasonable, material, and not merely an attempt to uncover defense strategy.[22] This mandatory reciprocity can be avoided by the defense by the employment of alternate means of discovering information, such as under the Freedom of Information Act.[23]

The Jencks Act[24] allows the government to withhold pretrial statements of any witness until that witness has concluded his or her direct examination at trial.[25] The act precludes the defense from "rummaging" through the government's files, but penalizes the defense by compelling the defense to bide their time.[26] A witness' statement is defined as a "substantially verbatim recital of an oral statement made by the witness and recorded contemporaneously with the making of such oral statement."[27] The Fifth U.S. Court of Appeals in *United*

States v. Edwards ruled that FBI "302" reports were not "statements" within the meaning of the act.[28] It is the defendant who carries the burden of requesting Jencks "statements," as demonstrated in *United States v. O'Malley,* where the Seventh U.S. Court of Appeals refused to overturn convictions for violations of the Racketeering Influenced Corporation Organizations Act, or RICO, and extortion, because the prosecutor had failed to turn over to the defense notes of interviews with government witnesses; according to the court, these "notes" need not be turned over to the defense since the witness had testified at trial, and furthermore since the notes did not qualify as statements under the Jencks Act.[29] Unfortunately for the defense the Jencks Act is the exclusive means of obtaining pretrial statements of government witnesses.[30] In *United States v. Polizzi* the Ninth U.S. Court of Appeals emphasized that point, for the prosecution failed to furnish the defense with (a) a statement made by a witness during his sentencing in an earlier criminal case, (b) the rough notes taken by an FBI agent during an interview with the chief government witness, and (c) the sworn affidavit of the witness provided in support of a motion for a new trial in the earlier case;[31] the court merely noted that the prosecutor had given the defense an opportunity to review FBI interview notes during trial, and that this gesture was sufficient compliance with the Jencks Act![32]

As delineated in Chapter 3, the 1963 U.S. Supreme Court decision in *Brady v. Maryland*[33] mandated that the prosecution cannot suppress information vital to the defense and that the prosecutor's failure to make any response is seldom, if ever, excusable.[34] In *United States v. Oxman* the Third U.S. Court of Appeals granted a new trial where the government deliberately refused to disclose an immunity agreement given to a government witness, the government contending erroneously that the immunity pertained to another criminal act.[35] In 1985 the highest court in *United States v. Bagley* ruled that disclosure of evidence that is both favorable to the defense and material to the guilt or innocence of the defendant must be disclosed by the prosecution.[36] The court defined "material" as a "reasonable probability that, had the evidence been disclosed to the defense, the result of the proceeding would have been different." Here the government failed to provide the defense with the information that two government witnesses had entered into a deal to provide information in exchange for money to be paid upon defendant's conviction![37]

The discovery process is the first step in litigation after the lawsuit has been commenced, and fortunately the discovery process has received the attention of many courts and has not been left to the discretion of the parties. In *Dynasty Apparel Corp. v. Lipton,* the federal district court dismissed the complaint and awarded judgment on default because the litigant failed to comply with many discovery requests, "a total indifference and failure to respond to numerous orders of this Court."[38] Similarly, in *Calajo v. The Italian Economic Corp.*, the plaintiff had failed to appear at a court-ordered deposition despite a warning that failure to adhere to the court's discovery schedule would result in a recommendation that the action be dismissed.[39]

A word on criminal procedure and the right to discovery: there is simply no general constitutional right to discovery in criminal cases.[40] The right to discovery in criminal matters is regulated by statute or rule.[41] Indeed, a court may prohibit defense witnesses from testifying at criminal trials to punish the defendants' lawyers for discovery violations. In *Taylor v. Illinois* the U.S. Supreme Court justified such harsh action as not violating the compulsory process clause of the Sixth Amendment if the defense lawyer's violations are aimed at gaining some tactical advantage or at concealing a plan to present false testimony.[42] In this attempted-murder case the defense lawyer did not seek permission to put a would-be witness on the stand until well into the trial, and the trial judge refused to allow the testimony as a "blatant violation of discovery rules." According to the highest court: "More is at stake than possible prejudice to the prosecution. . . . We are also concerned with the impact of this kind of conduct on the integrity of the judicial process itself."

2

ABA Standards for Discovery and Procedure before the Criminal Trial

More than a decade ago, the American Bar Association (ABA) promulgated discovery standards for criminal justice which essentially crystallize the general liberal principles of discovery.[43] Promotion of procedural efficiency, speedy and fair disposition of criminal charges, and a provision for sufficient information to make an informal plea and/or prepare for trial underlie the ABA discovery standards.[44] The thrust places the onus upon the criminal prosecutor to provide pretrial discovery to defense counsel, as particularly spelled out in Discovery Standard 11-2.1.[45] The prosecution must open its files to the defense and furthermore must accept an ethical obligation to disclose affirmatively information relevant to possible pretrial motions by the defense, such as motions directed to the existence of grand jury testimony which was recorded and not transcribed,[46] the existence of wiretap or electronic surveillance evidence,[47] or other evidence perhaps unknown to the defense.[48] The "open file discovery" represents a major concession by the prosecution and is consonant with the prerequisite that the prosecution must disclose to the defense, upon request, "all of the material and information within the prosecutor's possession and control."[49] It is self-evident that such requisite discovery facilitates the processing of criminal cases so that the speed and fair trial guarantees of the Sixth Amendment are assured.[50] The same liberal discovery requirements mean that the need for judicial supervision of basic discovery is minimized so that courts can devote more time to trial and other important matters. But the federal Jencks Act,[51] delineated in Chapter 3, restricts or limits discovery of witnesses' statements and grand jury testimony.[52] However, ABA discovery Standard 11-4.1 provides that "neither the counsel for the parties nor other prosecution or defense personnel shall advise persons (other than the accused) who have relevant material or information to refrain from discussing the case with opposing counsel or showing opposing counsel any relevant material, nor shall they otherwise impede opposing counsel's investigation of the case." Rule 6(e)(2) of the Federal Rules of Criminal Procedure, or FRCrimP, imposes a general rule of secrecy on matters before a grand jury, with certain exceptions, but there is no inconsistency here.

The defense also has obligations to disclose to the prosecution, and ABA Discovery Standards 11-3.1 to 3.3 provide guidelines. Sanctions for discovery violations are described in ABA Discovery Standard 11.4.7, and a general timetable for pretrial criminal procedures is set forth in ABA Discovery Standards 11-5.1 to 5.4. A prosecutor may not intentionally "fail to make disclosure to the defense, at the earliest feasible opportunity, of the existence of evidence which tends to negate the guilt of the accused."[53] The ABA Standards for Criminal Justice, to be differentiated from the ABA Discovery Standards, address the ethical obligations of the parties as to pretrial disclosure or discovery, labeling failure to comply with the discovery process as "unprofessional conduct."[54] Violation of the former can lead to disciplinary action against the attorney.

The National District Attorney's Association has also promulgated standards for discovery and disclosure, such as Standards 13.2(A)(1)–(2), and (3), which authorize the disclosure of the names and addresses of trial witnesses, their relevant statements, the defendant's grand jury testimony, if any, and the grand jury testimony of trial witnesses, if any. The mutuality of discovery is inherent in Standard 13.3, which mandates an "open file policy" by the accused, subject to usual constitutional limitations.

The ABA *Model Rules of Professional Conduct* also spell out the obligations of attorneys for both the prosecution and the defense in terms of "fairness" of conduct before trial.[55] Rule 3.5(c) proclaims that a lawyer shall not "engage in conduct intended to disrupt a tribunal."[56] Rule 3.8 deals with the special responsibilities of a prosecutor, and subparagraph (d) mandates that a prosecutor shall "make timely disclosure to the defense of all evidence or information known . . . that tends to negate the guilt of the accused or mitigates the offense. . . ."[57]

All courts are empowered to promulgate their own rules on discovery, and one of the most rule-conscious courts is the federal district court for the Southern District of New York. For example, effective July 1, 1987, the court adopted a new local rule that provided for uniform definitions and rules of construction in all discovery requests.[58] New Rule 47 provides precise definitions of "communication, document, [and] identify (with respect to documents, parties, and persons)," and also applies rules of construction to "all/each," "and/or," and "number."

There is obviously an ethical question involved in discovery, and it is contended by Professor Geoffrey C. Hazard, Jr. of Yale University School of Law that the deposition in particular may constitute a "modern day inquisition."[59] According to Professor Hazard, "when so much contentious effort goes into a process that may produce little and that leaves much to be desired, it is time to ask what is going on."[60] The *National Law Journal* itself points out that "irrelevant questions abound in many depositions. Lawyers often seem to use the process solely to harass their opponents. Sanctions against discovery abuse are limited, and few are meted out. In effect, many judges tacitly approve hardball litigation tactics during depositions as a way of winnowing troublesome cases. The area clearly cries out for fine-tuning. . . . The discovery process must be kept as open as possible, with both sides being given the opportunity to probe deeply into all relevant issues."[61]

3

The Discovery Process in the Federal Criminal and Civil Courts

FEDERAL CRIMINAL CASES

The 1963 U.S. Supreme Court decision of *Brady v. Maryland* had a tremendous impact upon the discovery process for it mandated that, irrespective of good or bad faith of the prosecution, the federal government may not suppress evidence favorable to the criminal defendant.[62] When requested by the defense, the government must provide that evidence which is material either to the guilt or punishment of the criminal defendant. There is an affirmative duty upon the prosecutor to produce such evidence as either direct evidence or as impeaching evidence.[63] In effect, the decision by the highest court established a minimum constitutional standard under the due process of law clause of the Fourteenth Amendment.[64] However, in its 1978 decision in *United States v. Agurs* the court drew back somewhat from its earlier pronouncement by stating that the prosecution's duty of disclosure is not violated unless its "omission is of sufficient significance to result in the denial of a defendant's right to a fair trial. . . . The proper standard of materiality must reflect our overriding concern with the justice of finding guilt. Such a finding is permissible only if supported by evidence establishing guilt beyond a reasonable doubt."[65] For example, the thrust here was to make certain that evidence which may substantially impeach the credibility of key government witnesses must be disclosed and not suppressed, including disclosure of promises of leniency or immunity provided government witnesses.[66]

Pretrial discovery in the criminal case is regulated by Rule 16 of the Federal Rules of Criminal Procedure (FRCrimP), and is predicated on the assumption that discovery between the prosecution and the defense occurs without the need for the filing of formal discovery motions or the involvement of the federal trial court.[67] Note that Rule 16 permits defendants to copy any relevant written or recorded statements they may have made, inter alia. However, certain information is not subject to disclosure, such as any "reports, memoranda, or other internal government documents" made by the prosecutor in connection with the investigation or prosecution of the case. Grand jury transcripts are also not subject to Rule 16. Rule 12 of FRCrimP permits the federal district court to set a date for the filing of pretrial motions at the time of the defendant's arraignment. Pretrial discovery is an essential device to ensure that the subsequent trial is speedy and fair.[68] As the highest court stated, "our adversary system is hardly an end to itself; it is not yet a poker game in which the players enjoy an abolute right always to conceal their cards until played."[69] The Fourth U.S. Court of Appeals in *United States v. Jordan*[70] had observed that the denial of a request for names and addresses of witnesses could result in a denial of defendant's right of confrontation in violation of the Sixth Amendment.[71]

The methods of discovery encompass depositions, both oral and written interrogatories addressed to the parties, requests for production of documents or things or permission to enter property, requests for admission of facts, and requests for physical and mental examination.[72] With the exception of the request for physical and mental examination under Rule 35 of FRCrimP, these forms of discovery have important common characteristics: they are designed to operate extrajudicially or without the involvement of the court; they require the signature or certification of the attorney requesting the discovery;[73] and they are, however, subject to court intervention, should it be necessary to protect the discoveree from undue annoyance, embarrassment, or harassment.

Rule 7(f) of the Federal Rules of Criminal Procedure permits a federal district trial court to direct the filing of a bill of particulars (which is truly not a discovery device) so that the criminal defendant may be better informed of the nature and extent of the criminal charges against him or her. Another purpose of the bill of particulars is to avoid surprise at trial and to protect the defendant from double jeopardy if he or she is prosecuted again for an inadequately described criminal offense.[74] Another tool which has some of the characteristics of a discovery device is Rule 17 subpoena duces tecum, which permits the attorney to compel prior to trial the production of "books, papers, documents, or other objects."[75] These subpoenas duces tecum enable a party to reach relevant material in the hands of third parties, but as expressed by the U.S. Supreme Court in *United States v. Iozia* the subpoena can only reach relevant material that is evidentiary and that is otherwise not procurable by the party reasonably in advance of trial by the exercise of due diligence.[76] Furthermore, the party must be unable to prepare for trial without such production and inspection, and the subpoena application to the court must be made in good faith and not as part of a "fishing expedition."[77]

The thrust of the foregoing involving federal criminal cases points up an essential difference from federal civil cases, as perhaps illustrated by *United States v. (Under Seal) (In re Grand Jury Subpoena),* where the Fourth U.S. Court of Appeals ruled that a federal grand jury's interest in obtaining evidence relevant to criminal investigation outweighed the value of a civil protective order in obtaining evidence in a civil proceeding, and therefore the grand jury subpoena requiring production of the civil deposition given under assurance of a protective order should be enforced.[78] The court stated that, besides hindering the underlying criminal investigation, a rule permitting a civil protective order to prevail over a grand jury subpoena might have other pernicious consequences such as preventing the government from obtaining important evidence that could be used for impeachment purposes if the deponent were to testify in a manner materially different or inconsistent with the deposition testimony in the criminal trial.[79]

FEDERAL CIVIL CASES

Discovery procedures available in federal civil cases are generally far more extensive than discovery procedures available in federal criminal cases (the dichotomy of the situation is disturbing, for the higher stakes in criminal cases should logically mandate greater discovery). Formal discovery in federal civil cases commences contemporaneously with the filing of the civil complaint. Admissibility of requested discovery materials is not the yardstick of permissible discovery,[80] as previously pointed out.[81]

Depositions upon oral examination, permitted by Rule 26 of the Federal Rules of Civil Procedure, or FRCP, must be taken upon proper notice if the deposition is to be admissible at trial.[82] The deposition may be accompanied with a demand for the production of relevant documents, with or without a subpoena duces tecum. A nonparty may be deposed outside the jurisdiction of the court under Rule 45(d). Depositions perpetuate testimony, can waive provisions of the "dead man's statute" (which precludes testimony by the survivor of a contract or cause of action), and can even waive subsequent incompetence of witnesses.[83] Rule 30(b)(6) places responsibility upon a corporation to identify that witness who will speak for the corporation.[84] Depositions upon written questions under Rule 31 are less expensive than oral depositions, but are hardly sufficient to elicit the requested information since the answers to the questions are generally supplied by the attorney and not by the client or witness. Written interrogatories are authorized by Rule 33: "an interrogatory otherwise proper is not necessarily objectionable merely because an answer to the interrogatory involves an opinion or contention that relates to fact or the application of law to fact, but the court may order that such an interrogatory need not be answered until after designated discovery has been completed or until a pre-trial conference or other later time."[85] Interrogatories seek to discover, under oath, relevant facts or to learn where such facts may be discovered.[86] Custody of relevant documents is also another purpose behind the interrogatory.[87] It is Rule 34(a) that deals with the scope of production of documents and things as well as entry upon land for inspection and other purposes.[88] Rule 35 establishes the conditions under which physical and mental examinations may be ordered by the court.[89]

There are many specific problems on discovery which relate to insurance policies, expert opinion, materials prepared for litigation, requests for admission, and attorneys' fees, inter alia. Rule 26(b)(2), entitled Insurance Agreements, states that "a party may obtain discovery of the existence and contents of any insurance agreement under which any person carrying on an insurance business may be liable to satisfy part or all of a judgment which may be entered in the action or to indemnify or reimburse for payments made to satisfy the judgment. Information concerning the insurance agreement is not by reason of its disclosure admissible in evidence at trial. For purpose of this paragraph, an application for insurance shall not be treated as part of an insurance agreement." Thus, plaintiff's attorney would be entitled to know the extent of defendant's insurance coverage involved in a particular case.[90] The disclosure of insurance allows the attorney to determine whether sufficient funds are likely to be available to satisfy the claim and also to determine whether the insurer is negotiating in good faith, based upon the applicable limits of the policy of insurance. Expert opinion disclosure is governed by Rule 26(b)(4)(A)(i), and the attorney may request that the subject matter upon which the expert is expected to testify be disclosed; also, the substance of the facts and opinions to which the expert is expected to testify should be available for discovery. Generally, the expert will not be orally deposed, for Rule 26 takes the position that discovery of the expert should be done by interrogatories. Materials prepared for litigation are not generally available for discovery unless the party seeking discovery can show a "substantial need of the materials" as delineated under Rule 26(b)(3). The so-called "work-product doctrine" simply does not work all the time, and certain work in preparation for trial may be discoverable.[91] Requests for admission can be served with the complaint or subsequently, and failure to respond may result in the court ruling that the requested facts are admitted.[92] Attorneys' fees are not usually the subject of discovery, although in *Bower v. Weisman* the federal district court for the Southern District of New York denied defendant's motion to compel plaintiff to answer questions on the fee arrangement with her current attorney;[93] the court found that, since neither party had argued that the issue of attorney's fees should be submitted to the jury, the subject matter was not discoverable.[94] On the other hand, implementing safeguards to protect the attorney-client privilege is one of the important duties of the courts.[95] The attorney work-product rule, as mentioned above, is said to protect the adversary system by striking a compromise between full disclosure to aid the search for truth and encouragement of effective legal representation by protecting a lawyer's mental processes and opinions from disclosure to an adversary.[96]

It should be observed that discovery orders are normally interlocutory and therefore are not readily appealable.[97] But if the proceeding pending in a particular court is whether a discovery order will be granted or not, then the resulting court order may be appealable. If the principal action and the discovery ruling are both under the control of a particular court, an order concerning discovery against a nonparty is deemed to be interlocutory as far as the discovering party is concerned, and hence not appealable; but the order is final as far as the nonparty is concerned, and is therefore appealable. The rationale is that the nonparty cannot take an appeal from the final judgment in the pending action, so that his or her sole recourse is an immediate appeal on the discovery order. The Interlocutory Appeals Act precludes appeal of a discovery order unless the discovery order presents a "controlling question of law" and the appeal will expedite the litigation.[98] When a party is cited for "criminal" contempt for failing to comply with a discovery order, the contempt judgment is obviously appealable; but "civil" contempt is interlocutory and not necessarily appealable.[99]

4

State Criminal Discovery Procedures

While most state criminal discovery procedures are similar to the federal criminal discovery procedures, it is well to note that there are significant variations in the extent and type of discovery permitted.[100] For example, most states make the disclosure of reports of medical and physical examinations as well as scientific tests and experiments mandatory; but some states include all reports made in connection with the case[101] while other states limit disclosure to those reports the prosecution intends to use at trial;[102] still other states leave disclosure solely to the discretion of the trial court.[103] Most states adhere to the federal rules and the ABA Standards with respect to the prosecutor disclosing to counsel for the criminal defendant all evidence as to guilt or innocence.[104] But Massachusetts, in *Commonwealth v. Monteiro,* ruled that prosecutors "are under no duty to report sua sponte to the defendant all that they learn about their case and their witnesses."[105] In Nebraska the defendant's request for copies of witnesses' statements was denied, but leave was granted for defendant to depose all of the state witnesses without any showing of either materiality or favorability to support the request.[106] An anomalous scenario in the Florida case of *Gant v. State of Florida* brought embarrassment to the state prosecution, which was found guilty of discovery violation that probably would not have occurred on the federal level.[107]

State criminal discovery processes generally give trial judges the utmost discretion, unlike the federal court judges who must operate within the parameters of the liberal federal rules. In *Taylor v. State of Illinois* the U.S. Supreme Court in January 1988 upheld a sanction by the trial court when the defense counsel apparently lied to the court about the availability of a witness.[108] It seems that after the prosecution's chief witness had testified, defense counsel informed the court for the first time that he wanted to produce a defense witness who had not been identified in pretrial discovery; his excuse was that he had been unable to locate the defense witness previously, but the trial court "learned that the lawyer actually had visited the witness the week before the trial began."[109] Angered by what the court called a "blatant" violation of discovery rules, the trial court here excluded the witness' testimony as a sanction. The highest court observed that "the accused does not have an unfettered right to offer testimony that is incompetent, privileged, or otherwise inadmissible under standard rules of evidence. The Compulsory Process Clause of the Sixth Amendment provides him with an effective weapon that cannot be used irresponsibly."

"Pre-suit" discovery is common, as illustrated in New York by Section 3102(c) of the New York Civil Practice Law and Rules, which reads as follows: "Before an action is commenced, disclosure to aid in bringing an action, to preserve information or to aid in arbitration, may be obtained, but only by court order. The court may appoint a referee to take testimony. Where such disclosure is obtained for use in an action involving title to real property, the deposition or other document obtained shall be promptly recorded in the office of the clerk in the county in which the real property is situated." Note that the above section does not contain guidelines for its use nor does it set forth criteria for its implementation; that has been left to the courts. This pre-suit discovery process in New York is especially useful in the medical malpractice context, for it enables the claimant to obtain the necessary medical records to ascertain if there is indeed a basis for the subsequent medical malpractice action.[110] While a patient in New York has a right to obtain copies of medical records from the hospital upon payment of a reasonable charge, a patient also has the right to photocopy records for himself or herself.[111] The same Section 3102(c) enables the claimant to take the deposition of a doctor or even a person who may not be well. The necessary caveat was well expressed by a federal court: "discovery rules are not a hunting license to conjure up a claim that does not exist."[112] The liberality of New York discovery processes is further seen in *Rosenberg & Estis, P. C. v. Stewart,* where the court ruled that "in weighing the competing interests of an attorney to his retaining lien (for his client's failure to pay the bill for his legal services), and a former client to disclosure of files needed to proceed with a claim of legal malpractice, the client's rights are paramount."[113]

5

Discovery Efforts from Business Entities

The discovery process is perhaps best understood by viewing the myriad problems of discovery efforts from business entities, the least of which is the protection of data from competitors. When a corporation is sued, finding directors and officers who will competently answer questions or adequately provide requested data is not an easy task for the party seeking relief.[114] However, Rule 30(b)(6) of the Federal Rules of Civil Procedure is designed to handle some of these difficulties;[115] in short, the corporation must name the person or persons to be deposed or otherwise to be subjected to some other form of discovery.[116] In *Cates v. LTV Aerospace Corp.* the Fifth U.S. Court of Appeals stressed the purpose of Rule 30(b)(6) as reducing the difficulty in determining whether the person deposed has the proper authority and is competent to furnish the requested information, thereby precluding squabbles over whether the particular officer, director, agent, or employee of the corporation has the requisite personal knowledge or familiarity with the requested information, and at the same time protecting the corporation by eliminating unnecessary and unproductive discovery efforts.[117] Thus, the burden of discovery rests more upon the recipient of the notice of discovery than upon the person requesting the desired information. The federal court in New Jersey in *Worthington Pump Corp. v. Hoffert Marine, Inc.*, for example, faced the problem of a witness for the corporation who invoked the Fifth Amendment privilege against self-incrimination;[118] all other officers, directors, and employees were "in the same boat" and all were fearful of potential criminal liability. The court found the corporation had failed to comply with Rule 30(b)(6) and thereby had sanctioned the adverse inferences to be drawn against the corporation itself.[119]

Hospitals are frequently involved in discovery efforts by patients, despite the fact that patients do have basic rights to their medical and hospital records.[120] In *Holder v. City of New York* the petitioner moved for discovery before bringing an action against the defendant hospital, whose allegedly negligent treatment of his mother resulted in her death;[121] the hospital's defense to the discovery effort was that some of the information requested might be privileged. But the New York court recognized the petitioner's right to "pre-action discovery" and ordered the hospital to produce all records and documents requested. The court, however, added the caveat that the petitioner would have to bear the cost of production of such records and documents.

Discovery and admissibility of prior complaints and incidents in the products liability situation is another common discovery problem with business entities.[122] The existence or absence of prior (and perhaps subsequent) complaints or incidents relating to the use or consumption of the product of the defendant is generally a proper and relevant subject for pretrial discovery.[123] The defendant's leading defense is the dissimilarity with the product or the incident giving rise to the claim of liability. In *Bihorn v. Lipman* the New York court ordered the drug manufacturer to produce the transcript of a meeting held 15 years before plaintiff's injury on the ground that the minutes of the meeting "might have been" relevant to the manufacturer's knowledge of the drug products' dangerous qualities.[124] And more recently in *Dean v. A. H. Robins Co.*, the court required the defendant to produce all documents containing opinions and reports of tests, examinations, or studies concerning the safety or characteristics of the Dalkon Shield product during the relevant time period, provided that such data or information was then available to defendant's officers, directors, employees, or attorneys.[125] The New York appellate court in *Mestman v. Ariens Co.* pointed out that "in products liability cases, disclosure has been permitted with respect to other claims against the defendant, similar in nature to that asserted by the plaintiffs, whether such claims were made prior or subsequent to the plaintiff's claim."[126] But here the record contained "insufficient proof that other predecessor models (of snowblowers) were sufficiently similar in design to sustain an expansive disclosure sought by plaintiffs." The court also ruled that "the relevant time period should have been limited to studies of competitive products in the market place and studies of cost analysis pertaining to the installation of an operator's presence switch that were made by defendant in the normal course of business . . . for the market years 1968 through 1971."

Discovery of prior and even subsequent complaints about the product has been denied where the requested discovery is irrelevant, overly broad, unduly burdensome, or the requested information is protected by privilege or the right of privacy.[127] The New Hampshire Supreme Court in *Farnum v. Bristol-Myers Co.*[128] placed restrictions upon the plaintiff's discovery by authorizing disclosure of only those complaints that were similar in nature to the complaint made by the plaintiff and which were received by the corporate defendant in the period ending when the company commenced warning potential users of the product of a risk in the use of the product.[129] Privileged information is also a bar to discovery, as illustrated in *Pollitt v. Mobay Chemical Corp.*, where a former employee of defendant sued the defendant chemical manufacturer and sought to discover all records of injuries to other employees;[130] but the federal district court held that the injured plaintiff-employee could not discover such records pertaining to diagnosis or treatment by company medical personnel because the documents included privileged communications between employee-patient and employee-physician. Even where the discovered evidence relates to similar complaints a trial court may bar introduction of such evidence at trial: "An examination of these reports reveals that some of them contain either highly inflammatory letters . . . relating to details of accidents, which would clearly be inadmissible. Plaintiffs made no attempt to limit or delete the hearsay portions of these reports. . . . We believe the prejudicial nature of the reports far outweighs any probative value they might have. . . ."[131] The fact of absence of similar complaints, it is argued, should be admissible evidence of lack of notice of any dangerous condition[132] or that the accident was not caused by the defect or dangerous condition of the product;[133] but this argument belies the fact that "negative evidence" rarely has probative value unless there is corroborative evidence in support thereof.

A party can waive privileges (and perhaps right of privacy) so as to enlarge the scope of the other party's discovery efforts, as shown in *Bower v. Weisman*.[134] Here the federal district court held that the prior production of certain privileged documents, including draft property settlement agreements between plaintiff and defendant discussed and negotiated in 1984, and letters from defendant's counsel to defendant's business and financial consultant outlining the purpose of the agreements and the reason for the various changes, was deemed a sufficient waiver of defendant's privilege to permit oral examination about defendant's communications with his counsel. The court also ruled that the defendant had waived the attorney-client privilege on the entire subject matter of his will and certain trust agreements by the prior production of his attorney's handwritten notes which reflected attorney-client communications about the preparation of those documents.

One of the major discovery efforts against business entities was sanctioned by the U.S. Supreme Court on November 16, 1987 in the case of *Dow Chemical Co. v. Ryan.*[135] Here, over the protest of seven chemical manufacturers of dioxin or Agent Orange, the thousands of Vietnam veterans who brought suit against the defendants were granted permission to see all research documents on the herbicide. The court order was granted despite the May 1984 settlement that had been reached establishing a $180 million fund for the claimants and their survivors, a group that totals about 120,000 persons. In resisting the discovery efforts, the seven companies had unsuccessfully argued that the ruling would encourage "frivolous suits for the sole purpose" of gaining access to private corporate documents.[136]

In *Parker v. Kawasaki Heavy Industries, Ltd.*, the defendant Japanese-based manufacturer of jet skis successfully shielded documents from discovery in a products liability case by invoking the protection of copyright.[137] In short, the defendant had copyrighted engineering and testing documents requested by the injured plaintiff, and the California court agreed with defendant.[138]

In summary, it should be self-evident that in the world of business, discovery efforts become most controversial because businesses simply do not want to disclose whatever data or information might conceivably be of value to competitors. But the competitive factor alone cannot be the basis for nondisclosure, as illustrated above.

6

Protection of Expert and Confidential Data from Dissemination

It was in the landmark decision in New Jersey in *Cipollone v. Liggett Group., Inc.* that the federal court proclaimed that "a protective order would favor the economically powerful defendants and prevent the public and the relatively impecunious plaintiffs from gaining access to material in which there was an enormous public interest."[139] What the court ordered to be disclosed and otherwise disseminated here was expert and confidential data about the tobacco industry which revealed that "industry researchers concluded 26 years ago that cigarettes contained cancer-causing agents, and that one company developed a less carcinogenic cigarette by 1979 but never marketed it."[140] The federal appellate court here vacated an "umbrella" protective order imposed on all discovery materials obtained from the defendant tobacco company; that protective order had precluded plaintiffs from sharing the data and the public at large from knowing the inherent dangers of the cigarette product. The vacating of the protective order did not necessarily mean that the protective order had trespassed on areas protected by the First Amendment. The court stressed that the burden of proving the constitutionality of information that the defendant cigarette manufacturer sought to protect rested squarely on the defendant's shoulders, on a document-by-document basis. The fact that the data did not contain trade secrets but only data, the disclosure of which could cause defendants "embarrassment," to say the least, was still grounds for protection under Rule 26(c) of the Federal Rules of Civil Procedure

(FRCP), assuming that defendant was capable of meeting its burden of proof.[141] If defendant cannot show that there is something worthwhile protecting, such as the "very heart of . . . business operations," then defendant is not entitled to the protective order.[142] It is up to the plaintiff seeking discovery to demand that the defendant, to defeat discovery, demonstrate cognizable harm such as economic loss or competitive disadvantage by the disclosure sought by plaintiff.[143] Once the data is discovered, it should be made available to others, as expressed in *Wilk v. American Medical Association,* which held that it is wasteful to require litigants in similar cases to duplicate discovery already made, unless bona fide litigants are readily able to utilize discovery from earlier similar cases.[144] Discovery of the identity of experts and expert witnesses as well as a summary of their opinions and anticipated testimony is essential to both plaintiff's and defendant's case.[145] In general, such experts and their opinions are discoverable if they are expected to testify at trial or if their information was not obtained in preparation for trial; an expert who was only informally consulted or who had been retained in anticipation of trial but is not expected to testify at trial, is not discoverable.

Rule 26(b)(4) of the Federal Rules of Civil Procedure spells out the unique limitations on discovery of anticipated expert witnesses.[146] And Rules 702 through 705 of the Federal Rules of Evidence establish the parameters for qualification of experts and admissibility of expert testimony in the federal courts.[147] It is up to the trial court to qualify experts and it is up to the jury to evaluate the experts and their testimony.[148] Expert witnesses can be disqualified when their testimony is "not generally accepted by the scientific community," as judged by the trial court.[149] Note that expert witnesses cannot be paid on a contingency fee basis, i.e., he or she cannot be paid more if the expert testimony brings victory.[150]

The work-product privilege of attorneys under Rule 26(b)(1) of FRCP, as well as the attorney-client privileged communication, often run afoul of expert testimony which seeks to hide behind these privileges.[151] In *Davis v. City of New York* the plaintiff claimed, inter alia, that he received poor ratings from his superiors because they are antisemitic;[152] the court denied plaintiff discovery and inspection of certain documents which the defendants claimed were prepared in anticipation of litigation, i.e., were privileged work-products of the attorneys. The documents apparently discussed the process and criteria through which the evaluations were conducted. The court refused discovery even though it was unclear that the lawyers had been involved in the preparation of the documents: "While the primary purpose of Rule 26(b)(3) is to protect the work of an attorney prepared in anticipation of litigation . . . work-product protection also applies to the parties to an action and their agents." The court pointed out that, while plaintiff had a substantial need for the documents, he could obtain their "substantial equivalent" through the deposition of the defendants involved in preparing the documents!

The cornerstone for obtaining discovery in federal action is Rule 26(b)(1) of FRCP, but the vehicle of "protective orders," found under Rule 26(c), constitutes the opposition to discovery requests: "Upon motion by a party or by the person from whom discovery is sought, and for good cause shown, the court . . . may make any order which justice requires to protect a party or person from annoyance, embarrassment, oppression, or undue burden or expense. . . .[153] Indeed, the protective order is the safeguard for the protection of the parties and witnesses in view of the almost unlimited right of discovery. Protective orders range from holding that discovery may not be had to specifying the manner in which discovery may be had or used.[154] As stated in *Delong Corp. v. Lucas*, "the protective order rule empowers the court in the interest of justice to control the degrees of disclosure of information by a weighing of the respective rights, that is, on the one hand the right of the plaintiff to a liberal examination and on the other, the right of the defendant to a protective order. Equity and fairness have prompted the foregoing disposition. It is the fervent hope of this court that the parties will approach compliance with this decision in a spirit of cooperation and thus spare themselves from future time-consuming applications to the court for directions and clarification."[155]

Enforcement of protective orders is shown in *Falstaff Brewing Corp. v. Philip Morris, Inc.*, where plaintiff's counsel failed to return certain documents in accordance with the protective order and the court responded by issuing an order allowing defendant's counsel, at plaintiff's expense, to investigate the circumstances whereby plaintiff's former counsel had delivered the documents to the plaintiff when they withdrew from representing plaintiff.[156] Plaintiff was thereupon ordered to pay a fine of $10,000, subject to a refund if all the documents would be returned within 90 days. The court order also warned the plaintiff not to make copies of the documents nor to disclose nor make use of the documentary material. Altogether, the plaintiff was ordered to pay $27,184.68. The point of the foregoing is not to treat a protective order lightly!

Information produced in a lawsuit in compliance with applicable discovery rules is not public information, but there are no restrictions within the Federal Rules of Civil Procedure as to what a litigant may do with such information.[157] However, as illustrated in *Tavoulareas v. Washington Post Co.*,[158] a court may supervise discovery by imposing restrictions upon the utilization to which discovered information and materials may be put. Under Rule 26(c) the federal court may order

> (1) that the discovery not be had; (2) that the discovery may be had only on specified terms and conditions, including a designation of time or place; (3) that the discovery may be had only by a method of discovery other than that selected by the party seeking discovery; (4) that certain matters not be inquired into, or that the scope of the discovery be limited to certain matters; (5) that discovery be conducted with no one present except persons designated by the court; (6) that a deposition after being sealed be opened only by order of the court; (7) that a trade secret or other confidential research, development or commercial information not be disclosed or be disclosed only in a designated way; (8) that the parties simultaneously file specified documents or information enclosed in sealed envelopes to be opened as directed by the court.

An appropriate example of judicial discretion in compliance with Rule (26)(c) is seen in *Tavoulareas,* where the federal appellate court held that a litigant's desire to disseminate information produced under compulsory process and subject to a blanket protection order was outweighed by the producing party's constitutionally protected right of privacy in not having the information disclosed.[159] The defendant newspaper's First Amendment claim was rejected by the court, which pointed out that "the litigant's qualified expression of interest" must be balanced against "the court's interest in preserving the confidentiality of private information it has supplied that litigant." Indeed, "the court must avoid unjustified intrusions on the producing party's privacy interests. The court can no more sanction public dissemination of private information absent a compelling reason than a federal agency can indiscriminately disseminate private information collected from citizens. Second, the court has an interest in preserving the integrity of the discovery process by encouraging full investigation of the disputed issues.'' The U.S. Supreme Court in its 1984 opinion in *Seattle Times Co. v. Rhinehart* found that a protective order did not offend the First Amendment rights of the party because the protective order was entered on a showing of good cause, was limited to pretrial civil discovery, and furthermore did not restrict the dissemination of information gained by the newspaper defendant from other sources.[160] The highest court observed that the rules authorizing discovery are a ''matter of legislative grace'' and that

> a litigant has no First Amendment right of access to information made available only for the purpose of trying his suit. . . . It is clear from experience that pre-trial discovery by depositions and interrogatories has a significant potential for abuse. This abuse is not limited to matters of delay and expense; discovery also may seriously implicate privacy interest of litigants and third parties. . . . There is an opportunity, therefore, for litigants to obtain—incidentally or purposefully—information that not only is irrelevant but if publicly released could be damaging to reputation and privacy. The government clearly has a substantial interest in preventing this sort of abuse of its processes.[161]

This issue of ''relevancy'' of the discovery information or materials was delineated in 1987 in *Lebhar-Friedman, Inc. v. Movielab, Inc.*, where the federal district court for the Southern District of New York observed that the standard of relevancy is that ''discovery shall be permitted where there is any possibility that the information sought is relevant to the subject matter of the litigation.''[162] Here, under Rule 26(b)(1), the court denied a motion for a protective order and directed the deposition of one of defendant's officers in an action to enjoin an election of directors on the ground of misleading proxy materials. The corporate defendant and the officer had sought to avoid the deposition on the ground of a prior, preliminary injunction enjoining them from soliciting or voting proxies: therefore, the requested information and materials constituted an unwarranted intrusion upon defendant's corporate activities and was not ''relevant'' to the instant action. But the court rejected this argument, pointing out that a deposition of the officer was reasonably certain to encompass matters relevant to the subject matter of the action, and that an inquiry into the board members' qualifications could be relevant to motive and could aid plaintiff in establishing defendant's intent to suppress a report allegedly omitted in the proxy statement concerning the board's lack of qualifications. In *Palmieri v. State of New York* the Second U.S. Court of Appeals emphasized the relevant argument in holding that the attorney general of the state of New York could not gain access to documents sealed by a federal magistrate as part of a settlement in a private antitrust action; the attorney general contended that he needed the sealed documents in order to go forward with his own official investigation.[163] The court noted that if the state of New York could demonstrate that there existed a "compelling need" or "extraordinary circumstances," then the state might be able to gain access to the documents.[164]

"Extraordinary circumstances" and "compelling need" are also relevant factors in considering whether an expert witness who has been retained in anticipation of litigation, but who is not expected to testify at trial, may be subject to discovery.[165] In *Ager v. Jane C. Stormont Hospital and Training School for Nurses,* a medical malpractice action, one of the defendant physicians propounded interrogatories to the plaintiff seeking the identity of and information regarding informal consulting experts of the plaintiff, and the plaintiff refused to answer on the ground that experts informally consulted are not discoverable.[166] Although the federal district court in Kansas held the plaintiff in contempt of court, the Tenth U.S. Court of Appeals reversed, observing that no discovery may be had as to the identity or opinions of an informally consulted expert unless there are "extraordinary circumstances." In short, the defendant physician must show that it is impracticable to obtain the information by any other means than discovery: "The Rule clearly contemplates a showing that a party has found opinions by others on the subject to be unavailable before he may obtain discovery from his opponent's retained expert who is not expected to be called to testify on the same subject. Defendants have made no attempt to show that they are without sufficient funds or information to obtain other opinions. . . ."[167] Thus, "exceptional circumstances" would encompass scenarios where the expert has information about an item, document, or thing that has been destroyed, substantially changed, or is simply not available, and where a party is unable to obtain an expert because so few exist or all available experts have been retained by the opposing side.[168]

A discovery order was at the heart of a subsequent civil action concerning the criminal trial of Claus von Bulow, who had been acquitted in a second trial of the attempted murder of his wife by injecting her with insulin. Her children then instituted a civil suit against their father, alleging common law assault, negligence, fraud, and civil racketeering violations. It appears that Alan Dershowitz, who represented the father in the successful second criminal trial, wrote a book entitled *Reversal of Fortune—Inside the von Bulow Case.* Here the plaintiff children sought discovery, and the federal district court found that the father had waived the attorney-client privilege by acquiescing in the publication of the book by his attorney; that waiver extended to the contents of the published conversations in the book, all communications between the father and the attorney, and all communications between the father and all other defense counsels relating in part or in whole to the published conversations in the book. But the Second U.S. Court of Appeals did not agree and vacated the discovery order:

> First and foremost the petition raises significant novel questions of law justifying the issuance of a writ of mandamus. . . . In our view, mandamus properly lies to review these issues of first impression. . . . We hold that the extrajudicial disclosure of an attorney-client communication—one not subsequently used by the client in a judicial proceeding to his adversary's prejudice—does not waive the privilege to the undisclosed portions of the communication. Hence, though the district court correctly found a waiver by von Bulow as to the particular matters actually discussed in the book, it was an abuse of discretion to broaden that waiver to include those portions of the four identified conversations which because they were not published remain secret.[169]

Thus, the federal appellate court restricted discovery to these conversations and communications which were not extrajudicial or which had not yet been placed at issue during the litigation. In short,

> extrajudicial disclosure of an attorney-client communication . . . does not waive the privilege as to undisclosed portions of the communications. . . . There exists no reason in logic or equity to broaden the waiver beyond those matters actually revealed. . . . Although it is true that disclosures in the public arena may be "one-sided" or "misleading," so long as such disclosures are and remain extrajudicial, there is no legal prejudice that warrants a broad, court-imposed subjectmatter waiver. . . . The reason is that disclosures made in public rather than in court—even if selective—create no risk of legal prejudice until put at issue in the litigation by the privilege-holder.

Therefore, the plaintiff children were entitled to attempt to prove in a subsequent proceeding that their father's assertion of the attorney-client privilege was misleading or otherwise prejudicial.[170]

The attorney-client privilege was raised in the decision of *Lex Printing Co., Inc. v. Schwartz, Klink & Schreiber, P.C.*, decided by the New York Supreme Court, New York County, on February 19, 1988. Here the defendant law firm moved for a protective order exempting it from producing time records in an action against it brought by a legal printer for nonpayment of the printing bill. The court first considered the attorney-client privilege:

> The burden of proving the existence of a privilege rests upon the party asserting the privilege (Priest v. Hennessy, 51 N.Y. 2d 62, 69 [1980]; Koump v. Smith, 29 N.Y. 2d 284 [1969]). SKS raises no specific instances of privileged communications in its time records and ledger sheets. Without such a showing, public policy favors full disclosures and outweighs SKS's vague assertions of privilege in regard to these documents, especially in light of the obvious relevance of these papers to plaintiff's case, and the fact that this information can be obtained nowhere else but through these SKS records (Priest v. Hennessy, supra; see also Rumrill-Hoyt, Inc., v. Perri, 97 A.D. 2d 951 [4th Dept., 1983]). Thus, SKS's time records and its ledger accounts pertaining to the work performed on the appeal are not exempt from discovery under the attorney-client privilege doctrine.
>
> SKS asserts that all correspondence between it and defendants Kashi and Ashka relating to the appeal is also privileged. SKS makes no distinction, however, between communications from the client to the attorney, and those from the attorney to the client. The attorney-client privilege was developed to protect communications from the client to the attorney, not the other way around. . . .

In denying the law firm's motion the court stated that the law firm's

> time records and its ledger accounts pertaining to the work performed are not exempt from discovery. . . . In sum, SKS shall produce at the EBT all its time records relating to the appeal; that portion of the retainer agreement between SKS and co-defendants showing authority for SKS to order the preparation and printing of the appellate brief and appendix for the Kashi v. Gratsos appeal to the Second Circuit; SKS ledger accounts showing how many hours of time were billed to co-defendants for all the preparation of the brief and appendix on appeal; any correspondence from SKS to co-defendants conveying information about the status of the appellate process; any correspondence

from co-defendants to SKS relating to the authorization to proceed with the appeal; any inter-office memoranda relating to (1) the difficulty in preparing the brief and appendices on appeal, (2) the bulk of the papers, (3) the length of time needed to prepare the appeal; and (4) the quality of the work performed by plaintiff. Settle order on notice.

The mere institution of a civil action lawsuit means limited confidentiality, according to the First U.S. Court of Appeals in *Greater Newburyport Clamshell Alliance v. Public Service Company of New Hampshire,* decided January 29, 1988. The plaintiff created a limited waiver of his attorney-client privilege over confidential communications relevant to the subject matter involved in the suit. In *General Foods Corp. v. Jay V. Zimmerman Co., Inc.,* the federal district court for the Southern District of New York on March 7, 1988 rejected defendant's claim that certain communications between defendant's president and an attorney who was the president's stepson-in-law are protected from disclosure by the attorney-client privilege. The court ruled that no attorney-client privilege existed, and therefore protection from discovery was not warranted.

Plaintiff sued the defendant professional wrestlers for injuries allegedly caused by defendants' negligence; and, in seeking discovery, plaintiff requested information on the business and promotional dealings of the defendants. Defendants argued that the information was confidential, and, if revealed to the public or to competitors, would cause irreparable damage. The New York Supreme Court, New York County, on March 21, 1988, in *Belzer v. Bollea,* ruled that discovery will be allowed, but the defendants were entitled to a protective order requiring that plaintiff not divulge the information to any nonparty. However, the court did slap the wrists of the defendant: "The court has noted that certain materials were submitted to the court confidentially. The court accepted these in the belief that it would show the nature of the materials as to which the protective order was sought. Instead, the moving parties annexed to their memorandum 37 pages of news clippings about plaintiff's attorney, supposedly to show his penchant for publicity or to reflect adversely upon him. This court rejects and condemns such a tactic."

7

Nonparty Access to Discovery Materials in the Federal Courts

Discovery materials in the federal courts are at times made available to nonparties or third persons having no interest in the particular litigation other than having access to the discovered materials.[171] The 1986 decision of the Third U.S. Court of Appeals in *Cipollone v. Liggett Group, Inc.* would appear to have resolved the issue by ordering the dissemination or sharing of discovered materials on cigarette smoking to other plaintiffs, their attorneys, and the general public.[172] But that singular court decision may not always be consonant with the goals of judicial fairness and efficiency unless there is "regulated" disclosure of protected discovery fruits to subsequent litigants and to the public.[173] However, the Seventh U.S. Court of Appeals in *American Telephone & Telegraph Co. v. Grady* had earlier proclaimed that "discovery must take place in public unless compelling reasons exist for denying the public access to the proceedings."[174] An interesting variation on the theme of nonparty witness access to discovered materials is the 1987 decision of the federal district court for the Southern District of New York in *New Castle County v. Hartford Accident and Indemnity Co.*[175] Here it was the nonparty witness who was subpoenaed to produce for trial certain insurance policy forms, but refused to comply unless the court issued a protective order that was opposed by the plaintiff and defended by the defendant insurance company. The nonparty witness argued that, since one of its central functions is to develop standardized insurance policy language, its function [without full opportunity for its insurance company membership to freely discuss and draft appropriate policy language] would subsequently be useless and at an end, for publication of the comments of its members would have a chilling effect on its very existence. The court agreed, holding that a nonparty witness was entitled to a protective order limiting the use of documents to be produced pursuant to a subpoena to "use in this litigation." On the other hand, in *United States v. Salerno,* CBS, Inc. successfully intervened to obtain access as a nonparty to a videotaped deposition of a nonparty witness.[176] The Second U.S. Court of Appeals ruled that "the common law right to inspect and copy judicial records applies to videotaped depositions of witnesses" and that the witness' privacy interests "were insufficient to overcome that right." Strangely, the court did not consider the First Amendment rights of the press and media to the requested discovery.[177] The overall consideration of courts generally is "the constant, growing tendency of litigants to frustrate the trial discovery process such as was done [by defendant here]; [it] is dangerous and chilling to a process which is geared toward a search for truth."[178]

The federal appellate court decision in *In re Halkin* held that a protective order on discovery material unnecessarily limiting dissemination is unconstitutional under the First Amendment, reasoning that such limits or restrictions on dissemination must be subjected to the same strict scrutiny as any other judicial order restraining freedom of speech.[179] Therefore, before issuing a protective order restricting the dissemination of discovery material, the court must find that the harm posed by dissemination is "substantial and serious," the restraining order is "narrowly drawn and precise," and there is no alternative means of protecting the public interest which intrudes less directly on freedom of speech.[180] Of course, the parties themselves may usurp the judicial function by entering into agreements or stipulations on the nature and scope of the discovery and the right or non-right to disseminate discovery materials. But courts will intervene where the agreements or stipulations of the parties fail to meet the "good cause" requirement of Rule 26(c) of FRCP.

Requests to modify protective orders[181] are proper, as illustrated by the *Grady* case,[182] where the Seventh U.S. Court of Appeals found "exceptional considerations" that warranted alteration of a protective order to which both parties had agreed, thus attesting to the fact that the party seeking modification of the protective order has the burden of proof. In *Olympic Refining Co. v. Carter*[183] the Ninth U.S. Court of Appeals reversed the district court's finding against vacating a protective order that closed the door to discovery materials in an earlier antitrust matter, and stated that protective orders are "subject to modification to meet the reasonable needs of other parties in other litigation."[184] Thus, the federal appellate court favored unsealing past records for present litigants because the potential for vexatious or obstructive discovery responses is thereby minimized. On the other hand, in *United States v. United Fruit Co.*, access was denied to a competitor of the defendant who could have utilized the discovery materials "devastatingly";[185] the Fifth U.S. Court of Appeals observed that modification of the protective order would have impinged upon legitimate confidentiality interests without countervailing benefit to the litigation process or to the public at large.[186]

In the products liability situation courts have been exceptionally liberal in calling for widespread dissemination of discovery materials so that attorneys for other claimants against the same manufacturer could collaborate:[187] "collaboration among plaintiffs' attorneys would come squarely within the aims of the Federal Rules of Civil Procedure—to secure the just, speedy, and inexpensive determination of every action."[188] In contrast thereto is *GAF Corporation v. Eastman Kodak Co.*, where the court decided against allowing plaintiff to transfer any of the discovery documents to the federal government, all of which documents could be used by the federal government in subsequent antitrust litigation.[189] The reasoning of the court was based upon the principle that government powers here should not be enhanced by the court or by private litigants, particularly since Congress had refused to give the Department of Justice broad subpoena powers.[190] However, the federal government may seek discovery documents and discovery information from any number of sources without judicial interference. It is not a denial of due process of law for the federal government to benefit from civil discovery, as illustrated by *United States v. Kordel*, where the U.S. Supreme Court held that the Food and Drug Administration did not violate the Fifth Amendment rights of its civil opponents when it simultaneously prepared materials for criminal prosecution.[191]

It should be noted that since the scope of discovery is usually broad, an opportunity is occasionally afforded some lawyers to indulge in various forms of psychological harassment of witnesses.[192] Degrading questions may occupy the time of depositions, particularly of third parties, and are permissible if the questions are appropriate and relevant to the issues in the case.[193] Where the testimonial evidence would not be admissible at trial, a protective order may become necessary.[194] But there are limitations on discovery, particularly of anticipated expert witnesses, as set forth in Rule 26(b)(4) of FRCP:

> Discovery of facts known and opinions held by experts, otherwise discoverable under the provisions of subdivision (b)(1) of this rule and acquired or developed in anticipation of litigation or trial, may be obtained only as follows:
>
> (A)(i) A party may through interrogatories require any other party to identify each person whom the other party expects to call as an expert witness at trial, to state the subject matter on which the expert is expected to testify and a summary of the grounds for each opinion. (ii) Upon motion, the court may order further discovery by other means. . . .
>
> (B) A party may discover facts known or opinions held by an expert who has been retained or specially employed by another party in anticipation of litigation or preparation for trial and who is not expected to be called as a witness at trial, only as provided in Rule 35(b) [concerning opinions of examining physicians] or upon a showing of exceptional circumstances. . . .
>
> (C) Unless manifest injustice would result, (i) the court shall require that the party seeking discovery pay the expert a reasonable fee . . . and (ii) . . . pay the other party a fair portion of the fees and expenses reasonably incurred by the latter party in obtaining facts and opinions from the expert.

8

Discovery in Arbitration

Discovery in arbitration, or arbitral discovery, may at first glance not appear to be salient to the informal, expedient process of adjudication known as arbitration. But it cannot be denied that a limited form of discovery is helpful to the arbitration process.[195] Arbitral discovery is governed by federal statutes,[196] state statutes,[197] court decisions,[198] and institutional rules such as those promulgated by the American Arbitration Association and other private institutions promoting arbitration.[199] In *Bigge Crane & Rigging Co. v. Docutel Corp.* the federal district court emphasized the value of pretrial discovery in arbitration as a truth-seeking, time-saving, and surprise-reducing function.[200] The court observed that where "the nature of any defense is unknown, the amounts involved are so substantial that any expense in taking depositions is relatively small, and the action has proceeded to such a point that the taking of depositions can probably be accomplished without delaying the arbitration," arbitral discovery is vital and necessary.[201]

The United States Arbitration Act[202] provides for limited discovery according to the discretion of the arbitrator, who can compel testimony from a witness and issue a subpoena duces tecum to produce any document, record, or thing which is relevant or material to the case.[203] Enforcement of the arbitrator's ruling is found in the contempt power of the federal district court. The Uniform Arbitration Act accords the arbitrator similar powers of discovery, but adds the power to depose witnesses who cannot attend the arbitration hearings.[204] Under the rules of the American Arbitration Association the parties can exchange evidence at the prehearing conference;[205] and Rule 30 thereof proclaims that "the parties . . . shall produce such additional evidence as the Arbitrator may deem necessary."

Arbitral discovery is admittedly time-consuming and probably not worth the concomitant delay unless the discovery is deemed vital and necessary by one or even both of the parties.[206] Frequently the parties may agree to avoid discovery if the amount in dispute does not exceed a designated amount. Arbitral discovery increases the fees to be paid to attorneys and others in the arbitration process. Where a party does not comply in good faith with a discovery ruling, such as by tendering incomplete documents, a court may even reverse an arbitral award, as illustrated in *Teamsters v. ABAD.*[207] In labor cases there is a duty to furnish information necessary to the negotiation of a collective bargaining agreement and the settling of grievances which arise during the course of the agreement.[208] In *National Labor Relations Board v. Acme Industrial Co.,*[209] the U.S. Supreme Court ruled that with respect to grievance arbitration, the employer must turn over to the union information and documents "necessary . . . to enable the union to evaluate intelligently the grievances filed."[210] In camera inspection is one means of protecting the disclosure of confidential information and confidential documentation.[211]

9

Discovery Outside of Bankruptcy

While bankruptcy itself has its own complex rules on discovery, the interesting inquiry is whether discovery may be had of the debtor in connection with an action pending outside the bankruptcy case.[212] Under Section 362(a) of the Bankruptcy Code "a petition . . . operates as a stay, applicable to all entities, of . . . the commencement or continuation, including the issuance or employment of process, of a judicial, administrative, or other action or proceeding against the debtor that was or could have been commenced before the commencement of the case. . . ."[213] Nevertheless, it has been held that Section 362(a) does not reach the issuance of process, such as a deposition subpoena, in an action in which the debtor is not a defendant. In *Johns-Manville Corp. v. Asbestos Litigation Group,*[214] the federal district court had declined to decide whether Section 362(a) automatically stayed all discovery of the debtor and its employees in all instances, but the U.S. Bankruptcy Judge temporarily stayed essentially all discovery against certain key officers, directors, and employees, noting that the thrust of Section 362 is to protect the assets of the debtor's estate from dissipation and administrative interference:[215] "The automatic stay . . . gives the debtor a breathing spell from his creditors. It stops all collection efforts, all harassments, and all foreclosure actions. It permits the debtor to attempt a repayment or reorganization plan, or simply to be relieved of the financial pressures that drove him into bankruptcy. . . . The massive drain on these numerous individuals' time and energy at this crucial hour of plan formulation in either defending themselves or in responding to discovery requests could frustrate if not doom their vital efforts at formulating a fair and equitable plan of reorganization.''[216] Thus, the U.S. Bankruptcy Court stayed discovery for seven weeks to coincide with the expiration date of the exclusive period for the debtor to file a plan of reorganization. The Fourth U.S. Court of Appeals in *Young v. Kerr Industries, Inc.* denied a plaintiff's motion to compel answers to interrogatories from a debtor in another case because ''to grant plaintiff's motion would interfere with the orderly administration of the reorganization proceeding.''[217] On the other hand, in *Norton Co. v. Johns-Manville Corp.*,[218] the bankruptcy court reasoned that the possibility of the discovery interfering with the bankruptcy was overstated and ''relatively insubstantial when assessed alongside the prejudice'' to the plantiff by denial of access to the discovery it sought.[219] In *Teledyne Industries, Inc. v. Eon Corp.*,[220] the federal district court for the Southern District of New York required the defendant-debtor to produce certain specific documents because this ''limited participation'' would not defeat the purposes of the stay.[221]

10

Discovery Abroad: The International Style

The discovery devices most frequently utilized in litigation within the United States to secure evidence are also utilized to secure evidence abroad.[222] But unfortunately the parties to the litigation (and the courts) often appear to disregard the fact that discovery of evidence abroad must necessarily affect the sovereign jurisdiction and domestic legal practices of those foreign countries from which the discovery evidence is obtained. The expansive style of American discovery procedures and techniques presumes "extraterritoriality"[223] and often results in the countermeasure by foreign countries of "blocking statutes."[224] In brief, foreign countries do not generally countenance U.S. discovery processes that infringe upon the powers of foreign courts, i.e., when the parties themselves handle the discovery processes without the intervention or supervision of the foreign judiciary. Pretrial discovery is sometimes confused with discovery prior to the institution of the suit, and many foreign countries take the position that "pretrial discovery" should be prohibited because it stirs up unnecessary litigation. In truth, the litigation has already commenced and the pretrial discovery is but an efficacious method of arriving at the truth before actual trial of the case.[225] England, for example, severely limits discovery by imposing upon the English courts the discretion to allow interrogatories or depositions; claims of governmental and legal privileges are, however, unusually broad.[226] Indeed, discovery is a veritable battleground in the continuing controversy over extraterritoriality:[227] "No aspect of the extension of the American legal system beyond the territorial frontiers of the United States has given rise to so much friction as the request for documents associated with investigation and litigation in the United States.''[228] Discovery processes differ materially in criminal law cases as opposed to cases in the civil law of antitrust, securities, and products liability, for example, but foreign courts do not necessarily appreciate the differences.[229]

Extraterritoriality is also a profound bone of contention between federal appellate courts, as illustrated by the liberality of *United States v. Bank of Nova Scotia,*[230] where the Eleventh U.S. Court of Appeals held that American discovery rules apply to *all* persons deemed present or having contacts within the United States, and *United States v. First National Bank of Chicago,*[231] where the Seventh U.S. Court of Appeals held that foreign sovereignty must be more respected in the foreign discovery process, so that extraterritoriality is entitled to less acceptance.[232]

While there is hostility abroad toward U.S. discovery processes, there is also antipathy for such substantive aspects as the pervasive U.S. antitrust laws and the extreme liberality of U.S. products liability verdicts and judgments. In *Zenith Radio Corp. v. Matsushita Electric Industries Co.,*[233] the Japanese defendants were compelled to make available to the plaintiff approximately 35 million documents in an antitrust, antidumping action.[234] And in *Wyle v. R. J. Reynolds Industries,* Inc. the Ninth U.S. Court of Appeals directed discovery from a nonparty foreign company, subject to requests or directions from litigants before the court.[235] The U.S. Supreme Court in 1987 in *Société Nationale v. U.S. District Court* ruled that the federal district courts may use the broad pretrial discovery procedures to their fullest extent in ordering foreign companies that do business in the United States to surrender documents and other evidence, even if those companies are barred by their own governments from complying with such orders.[236] This ruling is perhaps consonant with the concept of ''judicial sovereignty,'' i.e., all judicial acts are public acts, and only the sovereign can perform such acts; some foreign countries take the concept a step further by holding that the private performance of such public acts without the active supervision of intervention of the foreign country's judiciary is a violation of judicial sovereignty.[237]

A nondisclosing foreign party may attempt to justify his or her noncompliance with U.S. discovery processes by referring to Section 40 of the Restatement of the Foreign Relations of the United States, which provides:

> Where two states have jurisdiction to prescribe and enforce rules of law and the rules they may prescribe require inconsistent conduct upon the part of a person, each state is required by international law to consider, in good faith, moderating the exercise of its enforcement jurisdiction in the light of such factors as (a) vital national interests of each of the states, (b) the extent and nature of the hardship that inconsistent enforcement actions would impose upon the person, (c) the extent to which the required conduct is to take place in the territory of the other state, (d) the nationality of the person, and (e) the extent to which enforcement by action of either state could reasonably be expected to achieve compliance with the rule prescribed by that state.

The nondisclosing foreign party may therefore argue that disclosure should not be ordered because he or she would violate the law of his or her country, and thereby subject himself or herself to possible criminal penalties.[238] But it is another thing for the foreign party to conceal discovered information or documents from the U.S. court, as seen in *Timberland Lumber Co. v. Bank of America,*[239] and thereby impinge upon the U.S. national interest in enforcement of its antitrust laws.[240]

It should be observed that, in general, foreign countries follow an inquisitorial system whereby the judge conducts all proceedings from pretrial through post-trial. It is the judges who interrogate the witnesses, take the evidence after suit has been filed, and make the record based upon their own summary of the proceedings.[241] It is no wonder that liberal U.S. discovery processes are so "foreign" to foreign countries and tribunals.

The Federal Rules of Civil Procedure deal specifically with extraterritorial service on nonresidents: Rule 4(e), for example, allows federal courts to make service on nonresidents in a manner prescribed either by federal or state statutes or by the rules of the court of the state in which the federal court sits. But the basis of in personam jurisdiction must be found in the relevant state or federal statute or rule of the particular court.[242] While Rule 4(e) authorizes federal courts to use state statutes to obtain service outside the state in which the federal courts sit, Rule 4(d)(7) permits federal courts to use state statutes to serve the defendant within the state. Rule 4(i) prescribes five methods of service abroad: (1) service in the manner prescribed by the law of the country in which service is made;[243] (2) service directed by the original authority in response to a U.S. letter rogatory, provided that the service is reasonably calculated to give actual notice to the party from whom discovery is sought;[244] an application for a letter rogatory and for an authorization order must be made to the court in which the action is pending;[245] (3) service is made personally by a person, entity, or attorney who is not a party to the action by delivery to the other party, although the attorney for the receiving party can be designated to receive the process[246] (the caveat here is that personal service must also meet with approval of the foreign country where the receiving party is located);[247] (4) service is made by mail addressed and sent by the clerk of the court where the action is pending (a signed receipt is required, but even then some foreign countries frown upon this method of service as inconsistent with general principles of international law and constituting an infringement of the sovereignty of the nation where the service is made);[248] and (5) service by any method ordered by the court. Note that Rule 28(b) provides that depositions may be taken in foreign countries by notice, by commission, or by letters rogatory. Rule 29 allows the parties by written stipulation to modify the discovery procedures and take depositions before any person upon any notice at any time or place and in any manner.[249] But certain foreign countries have imposed their own parochial rules: Switzerland, for example, authorizes testimony only by written interrogatories embodied in a letter rogatory.[250]

A further word on England: only 5,000 practicing barristers appear in court in a country with a population of 60 million, compared to the more than 100,000 trial lawyers in the United States. The small number of lawyers in England is no accident; it merely reflects the place of litigation in English society. Social policy rarely comes before the English court, for social policy is exclusively within the province of Parliament. And in England there is no judicial review of legislative action, and English courts therefore cannot declare legislative acts to be unconstitutional. Also:

> If the company is sued in the United Kingdom, that executive can, in all likelihood, hand the matter to a solicitor and expect to hear next when the lawsuit is resolved. The executive's deposition will not be taken, no matter how directly his or her conduct is at issue. Even if the lawsuit challenges actions taken by the board of directors, those directors will not have their schedules disrupted by depositions.

Many American trial lawyers find much to admire in the English system of pretrial discovery. The English system is not ruinously expensive; in marked contrast to the U.S. system, the great bulk of legal expense is incurred at trial, not in pretrial maneuvering. Many of the discovery reforms recently introduced or proposed in the U.S. represent attempts to move its system in the direction of the English, that is, to make discovery quicker, cheaper, and less ambitious.[251]

THE RESTATEMENT OF THE FOREIGN RELATIONS LAW OF THE UNITED STATES

Section 420 of the Restatement of the Foreign Relations Law of the United States[252] recognizes the authority of a U.S. court to order the production of documents or information located outside the United States, and also recognizes the power of the U.S. court to impose appropriate sanctions in the case of noncompliance with such a court order.[253] But the discovery must be initiated by court order and not by a party's document or information request, notice of deposition, or other discovery request. The scope of discovery under Section 420 is limited to information or documents "directly relevant, necessary, and material to an action or investigation."[254] Section 420 states that the United States recognizes the general principles of international law by modifying Rule 34 of the Federal Rules of Civil Procedure to reduce friction caused by the application of Rule 34 to international litigation in situations where it was assumed that such litigation was identical to domestic litigation. Note also that under Section 420 (2)(b) "the sanction of contempt, dismissal, or default on the party that has failed to comply with the order for production" is less stringent than Rule 37 of FRCP, for the former requires "deliberate concealment or removal of information or . . . failure to make a good faith effort" before sanctions can be invoked internationally.[255]

When a conflict arises in which two or more sovereign countries have an interest, Section 419 of the Restatement steps in to address the scenario, as when a foreign country's command is inconsistent with the command of the United States.[256] The general preference of international law is that "prohibitions by the State in whose territory the act [of discovery] is to be carried out ordinarily prevail over orders of other States."[257] In contrast to the discovery practices in the United States, foreign countries, both in civil and common law, simply avoid asserting "long-arm" or extraterritorial jurisdiction over nonresidents, thereby practically limiting the possibility of conflict.[258] Even the U.S. Supreme Court gave its respect to a good-faith effort by a Swiss company in complying with a discovery order of a federal district court by not dismissing its suit: in *Société Internationale v. Rogers* the suit survived dismissal even though the Swiss company failed to produce documents "blocked" by a Swiss penal statute—documents which might prove crucial to the determination of the case.[259]

The American Law Institute, a private and voluntary association, in promulgating the various Restatements, seeks to clarify, rationalize, and thereby improve the law as it is interpreted by lawyers, the courts, and enforcement officials.[260] But the hub of the problem is that foreign nations simply do not subscribe to the liberal U.S. discovery processes, and foreign nations are irate over the extrajudicial application of the discovery process by U.S. courts. Section 420(1) of Restatement of the Foreign Relations Law of the United States sets forth the terms by which a U.S. court may require the production of information located abroad; and despite the criteria of reasonableness, weighing the importance of the information, the degree of specificity, whether the documents or information originated in the U.S., the extent to which compliance would undermine important interests of the foreign country, and the possibility of alternative means of securing the requested information or documents, foreign countries are still not willing to accept the demands of U.S. courts for discovery. Even "a more stringent test of direct relevancy, necessity and materiality" for discovery abroad does not satisfy the sovereignty of the foreign countries. Indeed, there is the stark fact that U.S. extraterritorial discovery is viewed by most foreign governments as a violation of international law![261]

THE HAGUE CONVENTION ON THE SERVICE ABROAD OF JUDICIAL AND EXTRAJUDICIAL DOCUMENTS IN CIVIL OR COMMERCIAL MATTERS

Drafted in 1965 and entered into by the United States in 1969, the Hague Convention on the Service Abroad of Judicial and Extrajudicial Documents in Civil or Commercial Matters,[262] known as the Hague

Service Convention, now has 24 contracting nations that have ratified it. It was the first time that the United States had approved a treaty on private international law.[263] The convention codified service of process by international registered mail, agent, and by formal request to a formal central authority, which agency must be designated by each contracting state to receive requests for service of process and to execute such requests for service of process. The central authority serves the documents either by a method described by internal law or by a method requested by the applicant, provided that that method is not violative of internal law.[264] Articles 8 and 9 of the convention permit the use of diplomatic consular channels for the service of documents or process (service upon foreign governments and foreign states in the United States is governed by the Foreign Sovereign Immunities Act).[265]

Compliance with the Hague Service Convention was the issue in *Newman v. Nissan Motor Co., Ltd.*, where the plaintiff moved for entry of a default judgment against the foreign automobile manufacturer.[266] The defense was based upon plaintiff's failure to comply with the convention, and the New York court agreed with the defendant that service of process "must be served pursuant to the requirements of the Hague Convention."[267] However, in *A. J. McNulty & Company v. Rocamat,* another New York court ruled that compliance with the Hague Service Convention was not necessary, for service of process was proper under New York law; both parties were foreign corporations and both parties were protected against suits without adequate notice under New York law.[268]

The Hague Service Convention does not pertain to criminal matters. Service by the central authority should be personal service wherever possible, although registered mail service in Japan has been approved by a California court.[269] Another acceptable practice common in European countries calls for transmittal of the document or process to a local police station, which calls the addressee and requests that the addressee pick up the document or process.[270] A contracting country must comply with the request to serve the document or process unless the request does not conform to the terms of the convention or the act of service would infringe on the sovereignty or security of the country to which the request for information or documents is addressed.[271]

It would appear that the Hague Service Convention is self-executing and therefore binding on federal and state courts.[272] In *Weight v. Kawasaki Heavy Industries, Inc.* the federal district court in Virginia proclaimed that the convention "has the status of a self-executing treaty, and thus, it constitutes the supreme law of the land."[273] And in *Voorhees v. Fisher & Krecke* the Fourth U.S. Court of Appeals pointed out that the Hague Service Convention "establishes affirmative and judicially enforceable obligations without requiring any implementing legislation."[274] Indeed, the convention does not create independent authorization for service of process abroad, but only provides a means of effecting such service.[275] The Hague Service Convention, being more specific than the Federal Rules of Civil Procedure, would prevail in event of conflict, at least in theory.[276]

Another international convention that is pertinent here is the Hague Convention Abolishing the Requirement of Legalisation for Foreign Public Documents, to which the United States was a signatory in 1981.[277] This convention provides a uniform method for certifying public documents that have been executed in one contracting state and that have to be produced in another contracting state.[278]

THE HAGUE CONVENTION ON THE TAKING OF EVIDENCE ABROAD IN CIVIL OR COMMERCIAL MATTERS

Ratified by 17 states including the United States, the Hague Convention on the Taking of Evidence Abroad in Civil or Commercial Matters,[279] also known as the Hague Evidence Convention, is an effective tool for obtaining discovery material abroad, except that under Article 23 thereof, where a majority of these 17 contracting parties have "reserved" their right to refuse "pre-trial discovery of documents," the convention sports a well-recognized loophole.[280] Article 1 of the convention provides that international judicial assistance for taking evidence abroad is limited to "civil or commercial matters," and that the letter of request for information of documents may be issued only by a court or tribunal of the state or origin to the judicial authorities of the state where the request is to be executed; the letter of request must relate to pending or contemplated litigation. Article 2 requires each contracting state (Barbados, Cyprus, Czechoslovakia, Denmark, Finland, France, West Germany, Israel, Italy, Luxembourg, the Netherlands, Norway, Portugal, Singapore, Sweden, the United Kingdom, and the United States) to establish a central authority (in the U.S. it is the Department of Justice) for receipt and execution of letters of request. The content of the letter of request is explicitly delineated in Article 3, and failure to conform to the explicit instructions can result in rejection of the letter of request under Article 5. The letter of request must be written in the language of the state where the letter of request is executed, as set forth in Article 4; but French and English are always acceptable languages. Article 9 spells out the fact that the state of execution of the letter of request will determine whether or not the procedure meets with approval under its internal law. Recalcitrant witnesses may be compelled to testify under Article 10 if such compulsion is proper and legal under the internal law of the state executing the letter of request. Privileges and duties of witnesses not to testify are not recognized in accord with the law of the state of execution under Article 11(1)(a) of the Hague Evidence Convention. Articles 15 through 22 provide that consuls and commissioners have the power to take testimony and procure evidence abroad; Article 23, the so-called "reservations" clause, has unfortunately been utilized by 12 of the 17 signatory countries.[281] Thus, the Hague Evidence Convention has limited international effect, for not only do 12 of the 17 signatory countries rest their laurels on "reservations," but worldwide application is not possible with only 5 of the more than 200 nations subscribing in toto to the provisions of the convention. Other restrictions on worldwide application of the convention include the right of a contracting nation to exclude service of judicial documents, issuance of any process for the execution of judgments, or the enforcement of court orders or provision for protective measures.[282]

In the United States the Hague Evidence Convention has fared much better since it is a treaty among nations, and therefore its provisions are binding on all federal and state courts.[283] The Connecticut court in *Cuisinart, Inc. v. Robot Coupe S.A.* held that the convention "represents the sole avenue open to an American party wishing to obtain evidence in one of the contracting states."[284] But that conclusion is not necessarily true, for Article 27(c) of the convention states that "it shall not prevent a Contracting State from . . . permitting by internal law or practices, methods of taking evidence other than those provided for in this Convention." A federal district court in *Philadelphia Gear Corp. v. American Pfauter Corp.* pointed out that "to allow the forum court to supplement the Convention with its own practices would not promote uniformity in the gathering of evidence nor generate a spirit of cooperation among signatories. . . ."[285] Another federal district court ordered discovery under the Federal Rules of Civil Procedure and not under the convention because it felt that the foreign plaintiff would be put to an unfair advantage otherwise.[286] The Fifth U.S. Court of Appeals in *Anschuetz & Co., GmbH. v. Mississippi River Authority* rejected the claims of the plaintiff and the U.S. Department of Justice that ordering depositions in West Germany without proceeding under the convention constituted a violation of West German judicial sovereignty and international law.[287] The federal appellate court pointed out that the purpose of the Hague Evidence Convention was not to restrict "the exercise of *in personam* jurisdiction by United States courts over foreign nationals properly before" the courts. In short, the Convention did not supplant the Federal Rules of Civil Procedure where the U.S. court has jurisdiction over the foreign resident under a state's long-arm statute.

The U.S. Supreme Court on June 15, 1987 in *Société Nationale Industrielle v. U.S. District Court* resolved the apparent conflict by proclaiming that the Hague Evidence Convention is optional and does not provide exclusive or mandatory procedures for obtaining information or documents or other evidence located in a foreign signatory country.[288] Here plaintiff's decedent died in an accident involving a helicopter manufactured by SNIAS, a French company, and the subsequent suit alleged that the death was caused by the helicopter's defectively designed or manufactured tail rotor system. Plaintiff requested production of documents under Rule 34 of FRCP, but SNIAS objected on the grounds that discovery must be conducted within the framework of the Hague Evidence Convention; furthermore, SNIAS argued that French law precluded the production of documents other than in accordance with treaties or international agreements. However, the federal district court ordered SNIAS to comply with Rule 34 of FRCP, and the Ninth U.S. Court of Appeals affirmed, holding that the Federal Rules of Civil Procedure govern discovery and that the convention was neither the exclusive nor the mandatory means for obtaining discovery abroad, especially when the federal district court has jurisdiction over the foreign litigant.[289] The federal appellate court also observed that United States' interest outweighed the interest of France which, at most, had a minimal interest in the proceedings because "no proceedings will take place on French soil."[290] It should be observed that Article 27(a) of the convention does give broad permission to the country where the evidence is to be taken to adopt other methods of taking evidence.[291]

In May 1985 there was a meeting under the auspices of the Hague Evidence Convention which focused on the relationship of direct U.S. discovery requests with regard to documents and persons located abroad.[292] But the U.S. Supreme Court in 1987 put those concerns at rest by proclaiming that the Hague Evidence Convention was intended to establish optional procedures for obtaining evidence abroad. To interpret the convention any other way would subject U.S. courts to the internal laws of the state of which a foreign national, subject to U.S. suit, is a citizen, according to the 5–4 majority of the highest court. Furthermore, "the exact line between reasonableness and unreasonableness in each case must be drawn by the trial court, based on its knowledge of the case and of the claims and interests of the parties and the governments whose statutes and policies they invoke. . . . We do not articulate specific rules to guide this delicate task of adjudication." The minority's dissent feared that the majority's decision "will resort unnecessarily to issuing discovery orders under the Federal Rules of Civil Procedure in a raw exercise of their jurisdictional power to the detriment of the United States' national and international interests." Accordingly, the minority "would apply a general presumption that, in most cases, courts should resort first to the Convention procedures." Where a foreign country is not a signatory to the convention, as was the case in 1983 with Japan, there is no problem, for the convention is simply not available, as illustrated in *American Honda Motor Co. v. Votour.*[293] But Japan subsequently became a signatory to the convention and, in a 1987 case, *Cooper v. Makita Electric Works, Ltd.*, the federal district court in Maine quashed the attempted service of process of the plaintiff upon the Japanese defendant.[294] In this products liability case, plaintiff made service upon Makita by registered mail sent to Makita's office in Japan pursuant to Rule 4(i)(1)(D) of the Federal Rules of Civil Procedure. Makita defended on the basis that the service did not comply with the convention. The evidence revealed that at the time Japan ratified the convention, Japan had objected to subparagraphs (b) and (c) of Article 10, which dealt with "the freedom of judicial officers, officials or other competent persons of [the United States] . . . to effect service of judicial documents directly through the judicial officers, officials or other competent persons of [Japan]'' and ''the freedom of any person interested in a judicial proceeding to effect service of judicial documents directly through the judicial officers, officials or other competent persons of [Japan].''[295] But subparagraph (a) of Article 10, which reads ''the freedom to send judicial documents, by postal channels, directly to persons abroad,'' was the real bone of contention; and the court ruled that the word ''send'' does *not* encompass the word ''service,'' and therefore the attempted service of process by registered mail was defective in terms of compliance with the convention.[296] But even where both parties are signatories to the convention, as with the United States and the United Kingdom, the highest court in 1982 in *Insurance Corp. of Ireland, Ltd. v. Compagnie des Bauxites de Guinea* ignored the Hague Evidence Convention in its zest for punishing foreign defendants who did not fairly respond to reasonable discovery requests.[297]

FOREIGN BLOCKING LEGISLATION

Discovery abroad can effectively be frustrated by foreign blocking legislation, i.e., foreign laws prohibiting disclosure of information or documents located in a foreign country or possessed by citizens of that foreign country.[298] In *Minpeco, S.A. v. Conticommodity Services, Inc.* the federal district court for the Southern District of New York observed that it has the power to compel discovery of a Swiss financial institution under the Federal Rules of Civil Procedure since it had personal jurisdiction over the foreign party and the foreign party had control over the requested documents.[299] But the Swiss bank secrecy laws precluded such discovery, and so the court expounded at length about the ''factors'' that should be weighed, to wit: ''(1) the competing interests of the nations whose laws are in conflict; (2) the hardship of compliance on the party or witness from whom discovery is sought; (3) the importance to the litigation of the information and documents requested; and (4) the good faith of the party resisting discovery.'' The court found that the balance of the ''factors'' weighed against directing the discovery. In short, the foreign blocking legislation prevailed over the U.S. discovery process because the Swiss had a stronger national interest embodied in the Swiss Bank Secrecy Act, which imposes penal sanctions on officers, directors, employees, or agents of a bank who disclose a customer's identity or any other information about a customer obtained in the context of the banking relationship. The court found that there was hardship in compliance with the discovery request, that the importance of the information sought by the plaintiffs had been reduced by waivers of bank secrecy already executed by "key players," and that the Swiss defendant was no longer subject to the drastic sanctions available against parties for disobeying a discovery order, that is, contempt and fines, which punishment "would be disproportionate under the circumstances and excessively harmful to international comity." It should be observed that the Swiss Bank Secrecy Act was enacted in the 1930s in order to protect the privacy and assets of victims of Nazi persecution pursued by Nazi agents.[300] Ironically, the first major U.S. legal confrontation with the act came in proceedings in which it was charged that invocation of the act was being used to conceal assets of Nazi interests held by a Swiss company![301] Where a Swiss company is found to have acted in bad faith, deliberately using the Swiss nondisclosure statute to evade the strictures of U.S. securities laws against insider trading, for example, the federal district court compelled discovery.[302]

In recent years, foreign blocking legislation has appeared in Australia,[303] Canada,[304] France,[305] South Africa,[306] and the United Kingdom.[307] The thrust of such legislation is to protect national commercial interests against what these countries view as unwarranted unilateral application of U.S. law, both substantive and procedural.

The "factors" delineated in the *Minpeco, S.A.* case are in conflict with some of the objective criteria as set forth in *Timberland Lumber Co. v. Bank of America,* where the court had difficulty in "balancing the interests" without any guidelines as to their weightiness or their international importance in terms of international trade and commerce.[308] It has been said that the presence of foreign blocking and concealment statutes adds "spice as well as frustration to transnational litigation."[309]

ARBITRAL DISCOVERY INTERNATIONALLY

Internationally, discovery processes are also found in arbitration, and arbitral discovery is a useful weapon in the arsenal of the parties to arbitration, although there is some reluctance on the part of the arbitrating parties, as well as the arbitration tribunal, in permitting discovery which could impede or delay the progress of the arbitration hearing and the timing of the arbitration award. Provision for arbitral discovery is found in the Arbitration Rules of UNCITRAL, or United Nations Commission on International Trade Law.[310] Rule 24 (2) and (3) thereof state that the arbitral tribunal initiates the discovery process, which may take place at any time during the arbitral proceedings. In addition, Rule 27 provides for the appointment of an expert to report to the tribunal "on specific issues to be determined by the tribunal," and the parties to the arbitration are required to "give the expert any relevant information or produce for his inspection any relevant document or goods that he may require of them." One of the limitations on discovery is delineated under Rule 24(2) requiring that the expert "invite a representative of each arbitrating party to attend any site inspection and, when the arbitral tribunal so determines, a representative of each arbitrating party shall be invited to attend other inspections made by the expert."[311] Any arbitrating party may request an order for production of documents or for the appointment of the expert.[312] Discovery in arbitration has been heralded as an effective means of uncovering relevant facts in the "search for the truth."[313] Noncompliance with a discovery order encourages the other party to question in court the finality of an award, thus undermining the efficacy of arbitration.[314]

In Rule 31 of its Commercial Arbitration Rules, the American Arbitration Association provides that

> the parties may offer such evidence as they desire and shall produce such additional evidence as the Arbitrator may deem necessary to an understanding and determination of the dispute. The Arbitrator, when authorized by law to subpoena witnesses or documents, may do so upon the Arbitrator's own initiative or upon the request of any party. The Arbitrator shall be the judge of the relevancy and materiality of the evidence offered and conformity to legal rules of evidence shall not be necessary. All evidence shall be taken in the presence of all the Arbitrators and of all the parties, except where any of the parties is absent in default or has waived the right to be present.[315]

The AAA Commercial Mediation Rules, on the other hand, deem mediation sessions to be private and the documents and information to be confidential;[316] there is no stenographic record,[317] and there appears to be no provision for discovery beyond what evidence the parties themselves introduce into evidence.[318]

The 1985 Rules of the London Court of International Arbitration maximize the powers and the jurisdiction of the arbitral tribunal, while minimizing the formalities and other restrictions which detract from the benefits to be gained by giving the arbitrating parties and the arbitrator the widest flexibility permitted by British law.[319] Article 5 thereof explicitly encourages the arbitrating parties to agree to procedural matters, for otherwise the arbitrator has the "widest discretion" to proceed as the arbitrator sees fit. However, Article 6 does provide for delivery of written submissions including evidence in writing, and Article 11 allows witness testimony to be presented in writing. Article 10.1, however, guarantees the right to an oral hearing, should either or both arbitrating parties so request. Under Article 13(1)(i) the arbitrator may in his or her discretion order a party to produce documents or other property for inspection; and Article 13(2) precludes any court of law or other judicial authority interfering with the discovery ruling by the arbitrator. Article 12, like UNCITRAL, provides that the arbitrator has the power to appoint experts, that the arbitrating parties have the opportunity to question such experts, and that the parties may present their own experts as witnesses.

It is interesting to note that several states have codified a requirement that courts may grant discovery in aid of arbitration only upon the specific request of the arbitrator when this request for discovery is made to a court having jurisdiction.[320]

Alternate resolution of claims is a modern arbitration procedure utilized in products liability claims, as promulgated by the Center for Public Resources in New York City.[321] Paragraph 2.3 thereof on discovery makes the point at the outset that "no discovery shall take place in this proceeding except as the parties otherwise agree," thereby raising some concern for the probabilities of abuse of the discovery process. Paragraph 2.3 continues: "Any discovery in this proceeding shall be expeditious and aimed at determining essential facts, without prejudice to the parties' right to conduct further discovery if this proceeding should fail to result in a resolution of the case. If litigation between the parties with respect to plaintiff's claim is pending, any discovery previously taken in such litigation may be used in this proceeding. Discovery taken in this proceeding may be used in litigation between the parties with respect to the incident."

DISCOVERY IN INTERNATIONAL CRIMINAL CASES

International criminal discovery does not necessarily follow the pattern of international civil discovery, for the obvious reason that the government is the prosecutor and the welfare and safety of the public are the paramount concerns. International criminal activity can be combatted best by cooperation among the countries of the world with respect to discovery, inter alia. Extraterritorial jurisdiction, or the power exercised in the territory of another country, upon which much criminal discovery depends, has unfortunately been declared to be in violation of international law.[322] However, judicial notice must be taken of international law, and the U.S. government, for example, is presumed to be bound to act in conformity with international law.[323] The pragmatics of the scenario frequently find U.S. court orders or subpoenas duces tecum at loggerheads with foreign court rulings and with the zealous sovereignty of the foreign country.[324]

The subpoena duces tecum is the principal discovery tool against international criminal activity. The subpoena duces tecum is the process by which a court requires production of documents, papers, or tangible things, and originated in the common law.[325] Issuance of the subpoena duces tecum is governed primarily by Rule 17 of the Federal Rules of Criminal Procedure. It is the clerk of the federal district court who issues the subpoena duces tecum, signed and sealed, but otherwise blank, to the party requesting it.[326] The clerk can issue the subpoena without a prior order of the court and even without a showing of the materiality of the evidence sought.[327] The party who objects to the propriety of the subpoena duces tecum must seek relief after the clerk has issued the subpoena duces tecum. Rule 17(c) states that the court, upon motion to quash or modify the subpoena, may grant the motion if compliance would be unreasonable or oppressive. Challenges to the validity of the subpoena duces tecum are generally made at the enforcement stage when civil contempt sanctions against noncompliance are in effect.[328] Provisions regarding contempt proceedings against a witness are contained in Rule 17(g): "failure by any person without adequate excuse to obey a subpoena . . . may be deemed a contempt of the court from which the subpoena issued."

Federal agencies frequently use compulsory process to force production of foreign evidence gathered under the federal grand jury subpoena duces tecum in criminal cases, as illustrated in *United States v.*

Bank of Nova Scotia, where the concept of extraterritoriality was approved.[329] Challenges to that procedure have taken the form of protests to the U.S. Department of State, application of bank secrecy laws or blocking statutes,[330] ex parte proceedings with foreign courts resulting in the exchange of judicial orders in conflict with those of the U.S. courts, and direct participation in U.S. courts on an amicus curiae basis.[331] In *United States v. Lemire* the U.S. Department of Justice sought evidence and investigative assistance in the criminal prosecution of the defendants from four foreign jurisdictions: Switzerland, Liechtenstein, Bermuda, and the Cayman Islands.[332] These U.S. requests met with widely varying degrees of cooperation, but it was the U.S.–Switzerland Treaty of Mutual Assistance in Criminal Matters that brought the greatest success.[333] It was obvious that bank secrecy laws can be used to improperly protect commercial swindlers, that sophisticated criminals use countries with such secrecy laws to delay and even frustrate legitimate law enforcement, and that foreign countries generally respond very slowly to criminal discovery requests. In *United States v. Marc Rich & Co.* the Second U.S. Court of Appeals upheld the enforcement of a federal grand jury subpoena duces tecum served upon a Swiss corporation by holding that personal jurisdiction existed over that corporation by virtue of its contacts with the United States in doing business in the United States:[334] "Where a person has sufficiently caused adverse consequences within a State, he may be subjected to its judicial jurisdiction. . . . It may well be that the occurrence of the offense itself [wrongful evasion of U.S. revenue laws] is sufficient to support a claim of jurisdiction, provided adequate notice and an opportunity to be heard has been given."[335]

It should be noted that the Restatement of the Foreign Relations Law of the United States provides much of the rationale for limiting enforcement jurisdiction in criminal matters.[336] The requisite of "reasonableness" is set forth in Section 403 (Tentative Draft No. 2, 1981),[337] and requests for disclosure and foreign government compulsion are delineated in Section 420 (Tentative Draft No. 3, 1982).[338]

THE MULTINATIONAL CORPORATION OR ENTERPRISE

The multinational corporation or enterprise, or MNE, is very much involved in the discovery process since ordinarily it must be responsive to the mandates of two or more sovereign countries.[339] The onus upon the MNE is most frustrating when the mandates of the countries are inconsistent and self-defeating; for example, the MNE may be a vital witness or an indispensable party to judicial proceedings in one country but is faced with a blocking or concealment statute in force in another country. Fortunately, the UN Organization for Economic Cooperation and Development (OECD) states in its guidelines that "when multinational enterprises are made subject to conflicting requirements by Member countries, the governments concerned will cooperate in good faith with a view toward resolving such problems . . . through . . . mutually acceptable arrangements."[340] The OECD Declaration itself suggests that "multinational enterprises should take fully into account established general policy objectives of the Member countries in which they operate . . . in particular, they should give due consideration to those countries' aims and priorities with regard to economic and social progress, including industrial and regional development, the protection of the environment, the creation of employment opportunities, the promotion of innovation and the transfer of technology."[341]

On the practical side, the federal district court for the Northern District of Illinois in *Westinghouse Electric Corp. v. Rio Algom, Ltd.* acknowledged its difficulty in weighing competing foreign relations with other political interests between sovereign countries, and therefore U.S. courts must regularly encounter nonjudicial problems in foreign discovery processes.[342]

In an excellent presentation on international discovery, "International Discovery After Aerospatiale: The Quest for an Analytical Framework," Gerber draws the following conclusions:

> The United States has chosen to utilize procedures to obtain information located abroad for use in civil litigation that most foreign countries consider unacceptable, at least under some circumstances. Nevertheless, because the United States depends on the cooperation of foreign states to achieve its domestic objectives, the analysis applied by its courts must reflect this interdependence.
>
> To the extent, therefore, that the U.S. legal system develops an effective mechanism for accommodating the interests affected by the extraterritorial application of U.S. discovery procedures, the system of international relationships on which the United States depends for achieving its policy goals will be improved and impediments to its policies will be reduced. To the extent,

however, that U.S. courts treat decisions on extraterritorial discovery as exercises in discretionary justice and/or consistently favor U.S. litigants or interests, United States extraterritorial discovery practices will continue to be a source of unfairness, conflict, uncertainty and waste.[343]

Notes to Part I

1. See articles by sociologist Robert K. Merton in the National Law Journal (March 17, 1986) at 10 and (May 6, 1985) at 3.

2. See Emanuel's Encyclopedia of American Law (1987 edition) at 127 et seq.

3. See Trial Magazine (August 1987) at 22 et seq.

4. Supra note 1.

5. See Jeans, Litigation (1986) at 160 et seq.

6. See Rule 26(a) of Federal Rules of Civil Procedure, or FRCP.

7. Note Kelly v. Kelly, decided May 9, 1988 by the New York Supreme Court, Queens Country: here plaintiff responded to defendant's 38 pages of interrogatories without preceding his answers with the text of each question. Defendant's counsel argued that such responses did not comply with the New York procedural statute (CPLR § 3134) and sought to compel plaintiff's attorney to retype or paste the questions before each answer. The court denied defendant's motion observing that "judicial intervention for so picayune a matter of form" was rarely needed.

8. See generally Note, "Managing the Discovery Process," For the Defense (April 1988) at 143 et seq.

9. 649 F Supp 664 (NJ, 1986), 785 F2d 1108 (3d Cir., 1987) and subsequently 802 F2d 658 (3d Cir., 1987), cert den 107 8 Ct 907 (1988).

10. See National Law Journal (July 20, 1987) at 6.

11. 510 NYS2d 870 (Bronx County, July 16, 1987).

12. "In light of the strong policy in favor of full disclosure unless the information sought is immunized, the burden of demonstrating confidentiality is upon the party asserting it (Koump v. Smith, 25 N.Y. 2d 287). The pro-

posed order would operate to impede disclosure by impermissibly shifting this burden to the party seeking to obtain disclosure of materials unilaterally designated as confidential by another. Moreover, it provides an extra tactical weapon of delay to any party who wishes to misuse this unilateral power.

Finally, none of the case law cited by Sportschannel would support a blunderbuss order of this character in any commercial litigation; indeed a preemptive confidentiality order of this broad sweep would be more suited to the Manhattan Project than it would to contracts for the broadcasting of baseball games. Public interest in this litigation is intense, and rightly so. Members of the general public are consumers of the product sold in various forms by the parties, and are concerned with that product's availability. Where the public's right to know damages a party's public relations, the damage done to that party is unfortunate, but is not a sufficient reason in itself to shield an entire case from public scrutiny.

Such an all-encompassing preemptive order would also be offensive to public policy, which favors public access to judicial and administrative proceedings (Civil Rights Law § 14; Judiciary Law § 4; Public Officers Law § 84 et seq.; § 100 et seq.). All judicial proceedings, both civil and criminal, are presumptively open to the public (Hearst Corp. v. Clyne, 50 N.Y.2d 707). Public access to judicial proceedings promotes public participation in government and provides a safeguard for the integrity of the judicial process (Matter of Herald Co., Inc. v. Weisenberg, 89 A.D.2d 224 aff'd 59 N.Y.2d 378)."

13. Unreported (SDNY, November 19, 1987).

14. See New York Times (January 11, 1988) at D2.

15. 88 FRD 674 (SDNY, October 14, 1987).

16. Note Rudow v. Cohen, unreported (SDNY, 1988) dealing with the difficult issue of attorney-client privilege where two clients formerly represented by the same counsel are involved in subsequent litigation. The federal magistrate initially observed that "the general rule is well settled that where two parties are represented by the same attorney in a single matter, communications made during that dual representation are not insulated from disclosure in a subsequent dispute involving the same two parties." The magistrate rejected defendant's argument that the joint-client exception to the attorney-client privilege does not apply because the documents sought were drafted after the plaintiff retained the services of another attorney. The magistrate ruled that defendant's act of retaining another attorney, to wit: his daughter, was insufficient to indicate an unmistakable purpose to sever relations with the first attorney.

17. See Rule 26(b)(1) of FRCP.

18. In federal cases the existence of privileges is determined under Rule 501 of the Federal Rules of Evidence. Note Byrd v. Blue Ridge Rural Electric Cooperative, 356 US 525 (1958).

19. Supra note 2 at 130–131.

20. Section 16(b).

21. See United States v. Opager, 589 F2d 799 (5th Cir., 1979).

22. See United States v. Estramara, 531 F2d 1103 (2d Cir., 1976), cert den 425 US 979 (1976).

23. See Freedom of Information Act, delineated in Chapter 13.

24. 18 USC 3500 et seq. (1984).

25. "The Jencks Act, 18 USC § 3500 (Supp. 1984), provides:
Demands for production of statements and reports of witnesses

(a) In any criminal prosecution brought by the United States, no statement or report in the possession of the United States which was made by a government witness or prospective government witness (other than the defendant) shall be the subject of subpoena, discovery, or inspection until said witness has testified on direct examination in the trial of the case.
(b) After a witness called by the United States has testified on direct examination, the court shall, on motion of the defendant, order the United States to produce any statement (as hereinafter defined) of the witness in the possession of the United States which relates to the subject matter as to which the witness has testified. If the entire contents of any such statement relate to the subject matter of the testimony of the witness, the court shall order it to be delivered directly to the defendant for his examination and use.
(c) If the United States claims that any statement ordered to be produced under this section contains matter which does not relate to the subject matter of the testimony of the witness, the court shall order the United States to deliver such statement for the inspection of the court in camera. Upon such delivery the court shall excise the portions of such statement which do not relate to the subject matter of the testimony of the witness. With such material excised, the court shall then direct delivery of such statement to the defendant for his use. If, pursuant to such procedure, any portion of such statement is withheld from the defendant and the defendant objects to such withholding, and the trial is continued to an adjudication of the guilt of the defendant, the entire text of such statement shall be preserved by the United States and, in the event the defendant appeals, shall be made available to the appellate court for the purpose of determining the correctness of the ruling of the trial judge. Whenever any statement is delivered to a defendant pursuant to this section, the court in its discretion, upon application of said defendant, may recess proceedings in the trial for such time as it may determine to be reasonably required for the examination of such statement by said defendant and his preparation for its use in the trial.
(d) If the United States elects not to comply with an order of the court under subsection (b) or (c) hereof to deliver to the defendant any such statement, or such portion thereof as the court may direct, the court shall strike from the record the testimony of the witness, and the trial shall proceed unless

the court in its discretion shall determine that the interests of justice require that a mistrial be declared.

(e) The term "statement," as used in subsections (b), (c) and (d) of this section in relation to any witness called by the United States, means—
   (1) a written statement made by said witness and signed or otherwise adopted or approved by him;
   (2) a stenographic, mechanical, electrical, or other recording, or a transcription thereof, which is a substantially verbatim recital of an oral statement made by said witness and recorded contemporaneously with the making of such oral statement; or
   (3) a statement, however taken or recorded, or a transcription thereof, if any, made by said witness to a grand jury."

26. Note the expansive view of the Jencks Act in Goldberg v. United States, 425 US 94 (1976).

27. Supra note 24.

28. 702 F2d 529 (5th Cir., 1983).

29. 796 F2d 891 (7th Cir., 1986).

30. See United States v. Covello, 410 F2d 536 (2d Cir., 1968), cert den 369 US 879 (1969).

31. 801 F2d 1543 (9th Cir., 1986).

32. Here is a typical motion by the defense to comply with the Jencks Act:

"The defendant, by counsel, moves the Court to require the government to produce all materials, within the scope of 18 USC § 3500 and Fed. R. Crim. P. 26.2, at least one week prior to trial.

In support of this motion, the defendant avers that early production will avoid the inconvenience and expense of recessing the proceedings during trial, pursuant to Fed. R. Crim. P. 26.2(d) to permit counsel to examine such statements and to prepare for their use in trial. To deny the defendant access to witnesses' statements in advance of trial, so that counsel can read and digest these materials, discuss them with the defendant, and find and prepare witnesses who may refute the testimony of the government's witnesses, will deny the defendant meaningful disclosure, deny the defendant his right to effective assistance of counsel, and impair the defendant's ability to prepare his defense, all in contravention of the United States Constitution.

WHEREFORE, the defendant respectfully requests that the Court grant the relief herein sought, and require the government to turn in all Jencks materials one week in advance of trial.

Respectfully submitted,

____________________ Date: __________

Attorney for the Defendant

Here is a typical motion for discovery pursuant to Rule 16 of FRCrimP:

"Defendants, by counsel, hereby move for a pretrial order granting discovery, and other relief; and in support thereof, the following is averred:

1. Counsel certifies that a discovery conference has been held on ____________with Assistant United States Attorney________________, that agreement could not be reached concerning discovery on or inspection that is the subject of this motion either at that conference or as a result of subsequent conversations; and that the defendants request a hearing to resolve the dispute.
2. Defendants request that the government be directed to furnish to them the discovery materials as hereinafter stated:
   A. The substance of any oral statement made by the defendants or any co-conspirators which the government intends to offer in evidence at trial. This request includes statements which have been related to the government by persons who heard the defendants or co-conspirators make such statements, as well as to statements made directly to agents of the government;
   B. Any books, papers, documents, photographs, tangible objects, buildings, or places, or copies thereof, which are within the possession, custody or control of the government, that (i) are referred to in the indictment; (ii) relate to any statement of fact in the indictment; (iii) relate to any element of the offenses set forth in the indictment; (iv) constitute the fruits or means of perpetrating any of the offenses set forth in the indictment; or (v) were presented to the grand jury in its investigation of any of the criminal offenses referred to in the indictment either as direct or circumstantial evidence of the offense charged, or in an effort to establish a motive for the offenses charged;
   C. All written or oral statements; or utterances, formal or informal, made to the prosecution, its agents and representatives by any person, which are in any way conceivably contrary to the testimony of that person, or any other person, whom the prosecution intends to call as a witness at trial, or which otherwise reflect upon the credibility, competency, bias, or motive of the prosecution witnesses;
   D. (i) The names and addresses of all witnesses who appeared before any grand jury investigating the charges set forth in this indictment;

      (ii) Transcripts of all proceedings before such grand jury, or grand juries, including the testimony of all witnesses;

      (iii) The date and nature of all proceedings before the grand jury, or grand juries, which was not stenographically, or otherwise recorded;

      (iv) The grand jury attendance sheets, for each date evidence concerning this case was presented to the grand jury, and for the date the indictment was returned by the grand jury;

(v) The record of the grand juries' vote on this matter that indicated the number of grand jurors that were present and the number of grand jurors who concurred in the indictment; and

(vi) The record of any summaries of documents or testimony presented to the grand jury;

E. All documents which relate to any and all evidence of criminal conduct, state or federal, on the part of any person whom the prosecution intends to call as a witness at trial, of which the prosecution, its agents and representatives are or will become aware;

F. All documents which relate to any and all promises, understandings or agreements, formal or informal, between the prosecution, its agents and representatives, and persons (including counsel for such persons) whom the government intends to call as witnesses at trial. This request includes such promises, understandings, or agreements that may have been made in connection with other cases or investigations;

G. All documents which relate to or suggest that any person who is a government witness, or prospective government witness in this case, is or was suffering from any mental disability or emotional disturbance, drug addiction or alcohol addiction at any time during the period of the indictment to the present;

H. All statements, oral or written, by the prosecution, its agents and representatives to any person (including counsel for such persons) whom the prosecution intends to call as a witness at trial pertaining in any way to the possibility, likelihood, course, or outcome, of any government action, state or federal, civil or criminal, against the witness, or anyone related by blood or marriage to the witness, or anyone associated in business with the witness, or any corporation, partnership, joint venture, or other unincorporated association employing the witness or in which the witness the witness has an interest;

I. All instructions as to the substantive law applicable to the charges to the grand jury and all instructions given to the grand jury regarding the standards of proof, credibility standards, and other legal standards to be employed by the grand jury, in the course of its deliberations. This request includes instructions given by any judge, government attorney or witness, orally or in writing and includes instructions as to the crimes actually charged in the indictment or as to charges which were rejected by the grand jury. To the extent that such instructions are found in transcripts of grand jury proceedings, the production of all such transcripts, in their entirety, is hereby requested;

J. All documents, including any memoranda, correspondence, standards, handbooks, guidelines, or similar materials which were employed by the government (whether or not employed by the government in this case) in making its determination to proceed in this case by presentment of the charges against the defendant to a grand jury instead of proceedings by way of preliminary hearing;

K. The names and addresses of all persons whom the prosecution, its agents and representatives believe to have relevant knowledge and/or information with reference to any charge contained in the indictment, but whom the prosecution does not propose to call as a witness at trial;

L. The date, time, and place of each utterance, statement, or action of the defendants and/or co-conspirators upon which the prosecution intends to rely at trial to establish any offense charged in the indictment;

M. The names and addresses of all persons said to have been present at, or to have personal knowledge of each utterance, statement or action of defendants and/or co-conspirators upon which the prosecution intends to rely at trial to establish any offense charged in the indictment;

N. The names and addresses of all government witnesses which the attorney for the government intends to call in the presentation of the case-in-chief, together with any record of prior convictions of any such witness which is within the possession, custody or control of the government, the existence of which is known, or by the exercise of due diligence may become known, to the attorney for the government;

O. All statements or documents, including grand jury testimony, and federal, state, and local tax returns, made or executed by any potential government witness at trial of this case, which the government knows, or through reasonable diligence should have reason to know, is false;

P. All documents relating to the authorization for the impanelment of one or more grand juries to investigate the offenses charged in this indictment, including the requests, and/or petitions, and/or applications, for such authorization or transfers;

Q. Any and all documents or transcripts which reflect evidence being submitted to the grand jury investigation of this case with an itemization, where it is not entirely clear from the document or transcript of the date or dates such evidence was presented to the grand jury. Any and all documents concerning the return of the present indictment, which reflect the number of grand jurors present when the indictment was returned and the number of grand jurors concurring in the true bill. Any and all documents or records including grand jury attendance records maintained by the Clerk of the Court, which reflect the identities of the grand jurors who were present on each of the days that evidence was presented on this matter, as well as the day the instant indictment was returned by the grand jury;

R. Any and all court orders, or other authorization obtained by the United States Department of Justice or anyone working with the United States Department of Justice for disclosures by the Internal Revenue Service of any return or taxpayer or taxpayer return information as those terms are defined in 26 USC § 6103, together with any application, affidavits, petitions, or other documents utilized in order to obtain disclosure of federal tax returns. In addition, detail any and all disclosures made by the Internal Revenue Service to the United States Attorney's Office or anyone connected with the investigation of any return or return information as those terms are defined in 26 USC § 6103;

S. Any and all court orders, or other authorization obtained by the United States Department of Justice, authorizing disclosure to the indicting grand jury of information obtained for the grand jury that investigated and returned the present indictment;

T. In addition to the foregoing, any documents, books, papers, photographs, scientific tests or experiments, tangible objects, written or recorded statements of any individual, grand jury transcripts, and oral statements of any individual reports, memoranda, names and addresses of persons, or other evidence or information which either tends to exculpate the defendant, or tends to be favorable or useful to the defense as to either guilt or punishment, or tends to affect the weight or credibility of the evidence to be presented against the defendants, or will lead to evidence favorable to or exculpatory of the defendant, which is within the possession, custody, or control of the government, the existence of which is known, or by the exercise of due diligence, may become known, to the attorney for the government;

U. Any and all medical records of all persons who the government intends to call at trial, reflecting either: (i) treatment and follow-up treatment for persons who the government contends were beaten, assaulted and/or physically abused by defendants, and/or any one of them, ostensibly under their control; (ii) medical records and/or history of any such person; and (iii) the name, address, and telephone number of each physician who has seen or treated such person within the last ten (10) years;

V. Any and all records of all persons who the government intends to call at trial, who the government believes were "unlawfully" arrested by defendants, or any one of them, which reflect their financial affairs over the preceding ten (10) years, including, but not limited to: (i) corporate, partnership and/or industrial income tax returns; (ii) bank accounts; (iii) stocks, bonds and other securities; (iv) financial statements; (v) W-2 forms; and (vi) 1099's;

W. Any and all records and/or testimony reflecting the employment over the past ten (10) years of each person who the government intends to call at trial, who the government believes was "unlawfully" arrested;

X. Each document or record obtained from defendant's employer in connection with the grand jury investigation of defendants herein;

Y. Each document or record obtained from the District Attorney's Office of the City of________in connection with the grand jury investigation of defendants herein;

Z. Each document or record obtained from the Police Department, District Attorney or court system which was presented to the grand jury; and

AA. Each photograph and results and reports of physical and/or mental examination, scientific tests and/or experiments in the possession, custody, or control of the government.

WHEREFORE, defendants request this Court: (a) to direct the government to produce the discovery materials and information requested herein for inspection and copying by defendant and his counsel; (b) for an Order setting a date upon which production of the materials and information set forth herein shall be made by the government; and (c) for an Order requiring the government to supplement its production of discovery materials upon discovery by it of additional evidence, information, and materials.

Respectfully submitted,

________________________ Date: __________

Attorney for the Defendants

33. 373 US 83 (1963).
34. See United States v. Agurs, 427 US 97 (1976).
35. 740 F2d 1298 (3d Cir., 1984).
36. 105 S Ct 3375 (1985).
37. Cf. United States v. Massa, 804 F2d 1020 (8th Cir., 1986) and United States v. Cortez, 757 F2d 1204 (11th Cir., 1984), cert den 106 S Ct 310 (1985).
38. Unreported (SDNY, 1986).
39. Unreported (SDNY, 1986). The court also awarded counsel fees and costs in the amount of $800.
40. See Weatherford v. Bursey, 429 US 545.
41. Note In the Matter of Miller v. Schwartz, unreported (Ill. Super. Ct., July 6, 1988).
42. 56 USLW 4118 (1987).
43. See ABA Discovery Standards 11-4.1 to 11-4.8 in ABA Standards for Criminal Justice, Discovery, and Procedure Before Trial (2d ed., 1980).
44. "ABA DISCOVERY STANDARD, 11-1.1 states:

Standard 11-1.1. Procedural needs prior to trial

(a) Procedures prior to trial should:

(i) promote an expeditious as well as a fair disposition of the charges, whether by diversion, plea or trial;

(ii) provide the accused with sufficient information to make an informed plea;
(iii) permit thorough preparation for trial and minimize surprise at trial;
(iv) reduce interruptions and complications during trial and repetitious trials by identifying and resolving prior to trial any procedural, collateral, or constitutional issues;
(v) eliminate as much as possible the procedural and substantive inequities among similarly situated defendants; and
(vi) effect economies in time, money, judicial resources, and professional skills minimizing paperwork avoiding repetitious assertions of issues, and reducing the number of separate hearings.

(b) These needs can be served by:
(i) full and free discovery;
(ii) simpler and more efficient procedures; and
(iii) procedural pressures for expediting the processing of cases.''

45. ''ABA DISCOVERY STANDARD 11-2.1 provides for prosecutorial disclosure:

(a) Upon the request of the defense, the prosecuting attorney shall disclose to defense counsel all of the material and information within the prosecutor's possession or control including but not limited to:
(i) the names and addresses of witnesses, together with their relevant written or recorded statements;
(ii) any written or recorded statements and the substance of any oral statements made by the accused or made by a co-defendant;
(iii) those portions of grand jury minutes containing testimony of the accused and relevant testimony of witnesses;
(iv) any reports or statements made by experts in connection with the particular case, including results of physical or mental examinations and of scientific tests, experiments, or comparisons;
(v) any books, papers, documents, photographs, tangible objects, buildings, or places which the prosecuting attorney intends to use in the hearing or trial or which were obtained from or belong to the accused; and
(vi) any record of prior criminal convictions of the defendant or of any co-defendant. . . .

(c) The prosecuting attorney shall disclose to defense counsel any material or information within the prosecutor's possession or control which tends to negate the guilt of the accused as to the offense charged or which would tend to reduce the punishment of the accused.

(d) The prosecuting attorney's obligations under this standard extend to material and information in the possession or control of members of the prosecutor's staff and of any others who have participated in the investigation or evaluation of the case and who either regularly report or, with reference to the particular case, have reported to the prosecutor's office.''

46. Id. at (b)(i).
47. Id. at (b)(ii).
48. Id. at (b)(iii).
49. Id. at (a).
50. See Warren Freedman, The Constitutional Right to a Speedy and Fair Criminal Trial (1988).
51. 18 USC 3500 (1976), and supra note 26.
52. Specifically, the Jencks Act prohibits the subpoena, discovery or inspection of any part of any report or statement made by a government witness or prospective government witness (other than the defendant) until ''after said witness has testified on direct examination'' at trial.
53. ''ABA STANDARDS FOR CRIMINAL JUSTICE, THE PROSECUTION FUNCTION, std. 3-3.11 (2d ed. 1980). This standard provides:

(a) It is unprofessional conduct for a prosecutor intentionally to fail to make disclosure to the defense, at the earliest feasible opportunity, of the existence of evidence which tends to negate the guilt of the accused as to the offense charged or which would tend to reduce the punishment of the accused.
(b) The prosecutor should comply in good faith with discovery procedures under the applicable law.
(c) It is unprofessional conduct for a prosecutor intentionally to avoid pursuit of evidence because he or she believes it will damage the prosecution's case or aid the accused.''

See also infra note 57.
54. Id. at (a).
55. See Rule 3.4 Fairness to Opposing Counsel:
''A lawyer shall not:

(a) unlawfully obstruct another party's access to evidence or unlawfully alter, destroy or conceal a document or other material having potential evidentiary value. A lawyer shall not counsel or assist another person to do any such act;
(b) falsify evidence, counsel or assist a witness to testify falsely, or offer an inducement to a witness that is prohibited by law;
(c) knowingly disobey an obligation under the rules of a tribunal except for an open refusal based on an assertion that no valid obligation exists;
(d) in pretrial procedure, make a frivolous discovery request or fail to make

reasonably diligent effort to comply with a legally proper discovery request by an opposing party;

(e) in trial, allude to any matter that the lawyer does not reasonably believe is relevant or that will not be supported by admissible evidence, assert personal knowledge of facts in issue except when testifying as a witness, or state a personal opinion as to the justness of a cause, the credibility of a witness, the culpability of a civil litigant or the guilt or innocence of an accused; or

(f) request a person other than a client to refrain from voluntarily giving relevant information to another party unless:
   (1) the person is a relative or an employee or other agent of a client: and
   (2) the lawyer reasonably believes that the person's interests will not be adversely affected by the refraining from giving such information."

56. "Rule 3.5 Impartiality and Decorum of the Tribunal
A lawyer shall not:

(a) seek to influence a judge, juror, prospective juror or other official by means prohibited by law;
(b) communicate ex parte with such a person except as permitted by law; or
(c) engage in conduct intended to disrupt a tribunal."

57. "Rule 3.8 Special Responsibilities of a Prosecutor
The prosecutor in a criminal case shall:

(a) refrain from prosecuting a charge that the prosecutor knows is not supported by probable cause;
(b) make reasonable efforts to assure that the accused has been advised of the right to, and the procedure for obtaining, counsel and has been given reasonable opportunity to obtain counsel;
(c) not seek to obtain from an unrepresented accused a waiver of important pretrial rights, such as the right to a preliminary hearing;
(d) make timely disclosure to the defense of all evidence or information known to the prosecutor that tends to negate the guilt of the accused or mitigates the offense, and, in connection with sentencing, disclose to the defense and to the tribunal all unprivileged mitigating information known to the prosecutor, except when the prosecutor is relieved of this responsibility by a protective order of the tribunal; and
(e) exercise reasonable care to prevent investigators, law enforcement personnel, employees or other persons assisting or associated with the prosecutor in a criminal case from making an extrajudicial statement that the prosecutor would be prohibited from making under Rule 3.6."

58. ''Rule 47: Uniform Definitions in Discovery Requests.

(a) the full text of the definitions and rules of construction set forth in paragraph (c) and (d) is deemed incorporated by reference into all discovery requests, but shall not preclude (i) the definition of other terms specific to the particular litigation, (ii) the use of abbreviations or (iii) a more narrow definition of a term defined in paragraph (c).
(b) This Rule is not intended to broaden or narrow the scope of discovery permitted by the Federal Rules of Civil Procedure for the United States District Courts.
(c) The following definitions apply to all discovery requests:
  (1) *Communication*. The term 'communication' means the transmittal of information (in the form of facts, ideas, inquiries or otherwise).
  (2) *Document*. The term 'document' is defined to be synonymous in meaning and equal in scope to the usage of this term in Federal Rule of Civil Procedure 34(a). A draft of non-identical copy is a separate document within the meaning of this term.
  (3) *Identify (With Respect to Persons)*. When referring to a person, 'to identify' means to give, to the extent known, the person's full name, present or last known address, and when referring to a natural person, additionally, the present or last known place of employment. Once a person has been identified in accordance with this subparagraph, only the name of that person need be listed in response to subsequent discovery requesting the identification of that person.
  (4) *Identify (With Respect to Documents)*. When referring to documents, 'to identify' means to give, to the extent known, the (i) type of document; (ii) general subject matter; (iii) date of the document; and (iv) author(s), addressee(s) and recipient(s).
  (5) *Parties*. The terms 'plaintiff' and 'defendant' as well as a party's full or abbreviated name or a pronoun referring to a party mean the party and, where applicable, its officers, directors, employees, partners, corporate parent, subsidiaries or affiliates. This definition is not intended to impose a discovery obligation on any person who is not a party to the litigation.
  (6) *Person*. The term 'person' is defined as any natural person or any business, legal or governmental entity or association.
  (7) *Concerning*. The term 'concerning' means relating to, referring to, describing, evidencing or constituting.
(d) The following rules of construction apply to all discovery requests:
  (1) *All/Each*. The terms 'all' and 'each' shall be construed as all and each.
  (2) *And/Or*. The connectives 'and' and 'or' shall be construed either disjunctively or conjunctively as necessary to bring within the scope of

the discovery request all responses that might otherwise be construed to be outside of its scope.

(3) *Number*. The use of the singular form of any word includes the plural and vice versa.''

59. See National Law Journal (March 14, 1988) at 13.
60. Id.
61. Id at 12.
62. 373 US 83 (1963).
63. Supra note 5 at 283.
64. See Freedman, Constitutional Right.
65. 427 US 97 (1976). The highest court continued: ''It necessarily follows that if the omitted evidence creates a reasonable doubt that did not otherwise exist, constitutional error has been committed. This means that the omission must be evaluated in the context of the entire record. If there is no reasonable doubt about guilt whether or not the additional evidence is considered, there is no justification for a new trial. On the other hand, if the verdict is already of questionable validity, additional evidence of relatively minor importance might be sufficient to create a reasonable doubt.''
66. See United States v. Crowell, 586 F2d 1020 (4th Cir., 1978), cert den 430 US 969 (1979), and Giglio v. United States, 405 US 150 (1972).
67. ''Rule 16. Discovery and Inspection

(a) Disclosure of Evidence by the Government

(1) Information Subject to Disclosure.

(A) Statement of Defendant. Upon request of a defendant the government shall permit the defendant to inspect and copy or photograph: any relevant written or recorded statements .nade by the defendant, or copies thereof, within the possession, custody or control of the government, the existence of which is known, or by the exercise of due diligence may become known, to the attorney for the government; the substance of any oral statement which the government intends to offer in evidence at the trial made by the defendant whether before of after arrest in response to interrogation by any person then known to the defendant to be a government agent; and recorded testimony of the defendant before a grand jury which relates to the offense charged. Where the defendant is a corporation, partnership, association or labor union, the court may grant the defendant, upon its motion, discovery of relevant recorded testimony of any witness before a grand jury who (1) was, at the time of his testimony, so situated as an officer or employee as to have been able legally to bind the defendant in respect to conduct constituting the offense, or

(2) was, at the time of the offense, personally involved in the alleged conduct constituting the offense and so situated as an officer or employee as to have been able legally to bind the defendant in respect to that alleged conduct in which he was involved.

(B) Defendant's Prior Record. Upon request of the defendant, the government shall furnish to the defendant such copy of his prior criminal record, if any, as is within the possession, custody, or control of the government, the existence of which is known, or by the exercise of due diligence may become known, to the attorney for the government.

(C) Documents and Tangible Objects. Upon request of the defendant the government shall permit the defendant to inspect and copy or photograph books, papers, documents, photographs, tangible objects, buildings or places, or copies or portions thereof, which are within the possession, custody or control of the government, and which are material to the preparation of his defense or are intended for use by the government as evidence in chief at the trial, or were obtained from or belong to the defendant.

(D) Reports of Examinations and Tests. Upon request of a defendant the government shall permit the defendant to inspect and copy or photograph any results or reports of physical or mental examinations, and of scientific tests or experiments, or copies thereof, which are within the possession, custody, or control of the government, the existence of which is known, or by the exercise of due diligence may become known, to the attorney for the government, and which are material to the preparation of the defense or are intended for use by the government as evidence in chief at the trial.

(2) Information Not Subject to Disclosure. Except as provided in paragraphs (A), (B), and (D) of subdivision (a)(1), this rule does not authorize the discovery or inspection of reports, memoranda, or other internal government documents made by the attorney for the government or other government agents in connection with the investigation or prosecution of the case, or of statements made by government witnesses except as provided in 18 USC § 3500.

(3) Grand Jury Transcripts. Except as provided in Rules 6, 12(i) and 26.2, and subdivision (a)(1)(A) of this rule, these rules do not relate to discovery or inspection of recorded proceedings of a grand jury.

[(4) Failure to Call Witness.] (Deleted Dec. 12, 1975)

(b) Disclosure of Evidence by the Defendant.

(1) Information Subject to Disclosure.

(A) Documents and Tangible Objects. If the defendant requests disclosure under subdivision (a)(1)(C) or (D) of this rule, upon compliance with such request by the government, the defendant, on request of the government, shall permit the government to inspect and copy or photograph books, papers, documents, photographs, tangible objects, or copies or portions thereof, which are within the possession, custody, or control of the defendant and which the defendant intends to introduce as evidence in chief at the trial.

(B) Reports of Examinations and Tests. If the defendant requests disclosure under subdivision (a)(1)(C) or (D) of this rule, upon compliance with such request by the government, the defendant, on request of the government, shall permit the government to inspect and copy or photograph any results or reports of physical or mental examinations and of scientific tests or experiments made in connection with the particular case, or copies thereof, within the possession or control of the defendant, which the defendant intends to introduce as evidence in chief at the trial or which were prepared by a witness whom the defendant intends to call at the trial when the results or reports relate to his testimony.

(2) Information Not Subject to Disclosure. Except as to scientific or medical reports, this subdivision does not authorize the discovery or inspection of reports, memoranda, or other internal defense documents made by the defendant, or his attorneys or agents in connection with the investigation or defense of the case, or of statements made by the defendant, or by government or defense witnesses, or by prospective government or defense witnesses, to the defendant, his agents or attorneys.

[(3) Failure to Call Witness] (Deleted Dec. 12, 1975)

(c) Continuing Duty to Disclose. If, prior to or during trial, a party discovers additional evidence or material previously requested or ordered, which is subject to discovery or inspection under this rule, he shall promptly notify the other party or his attorney or the court of the existence of the additional evidence or material.

(d) Regulation of Discovery.

(1) Protective and Modifying Orders. Upon a sufficient showing the court may at any time order that the discovery or inspection be denied, restricted, or deferred, or make such other order as appropriate. Upon motion by a party, the court may permit the party to make such showing, in whole or in part, in the form of a written statement to be inspected by the judge alone. If the court enters an order granting relief following such an ex parte showing, the entire text of the party's statement shall be sealed and preserved in the records of the court to be made available to the appellate court in the event of an appeal.

(2) Failure to Comply With a Request. If at any time during the course of the proceedings it is brought to the attention of the court that a party has failed to comply with this rule, the court may order such party to permit the discovery or inspection, grant a continuance, or prohibit the party from introducing evidence not disclosed, or it may enter such other order as it deems just under the circumstances. The court may specify the time, place and manner of making the discovery and inspection and may prescribe such terms and conditions as are just.

(e) Alibi Witnesses. Discovery of alibi witnesses is governed by Rule 12.1."

68. Note Dennis v. United States, 384 US 835 (1966) where the court deplored "the exclusive access to a storehouse of relevant facts" of the prosecution.

69. See Williams v. State of Florida, 399 US 78 (1972) at 82.

70. 466 F2d 99 (4th Cir., 1972).

71. Supra note 50.

72. Supra note 6.

73. See Rule 26(g) of FRCrimP.

74. See United States v. Carrier, 672 F2d 300 (2d Cir., 1981), cert den 457 US 1139 (1982). Note—"FED. R. CRIM. P. 7(f) states: Bill of Particulars. The court may direct the filing of a bill of particulars. A motion for a bill of particulars may be made before arraignment or within ten days after arraignment or at such later time as the court may permit. A bill of particulars may be amended at any time subject to such conditions as justice requires."

75. "FED. R. CRIM. P. 17 provides in pertinent part:

(c) For Production of Documentary Evidence and of Objects. A subpoena may also command the person to whom it is directed to produce the books, papers, documents or other objects designated therein. The court on motion made promptly may quash or modify the subpoena if compliance would be unreasonable or oppressive. The court may direct that books, papers, documents or objects designated in the subpoena be produced before the court at a time prior to the trial or prior to the time when they are to be offered in evidence and may upon their production permit the books, papers, documents or objects or portions thereof to be inspected by the parties and their attorneys."

76. 13 FRD 335 (SDNY, 1952).

77. See Hickman v. Taylor, 29 US 495 (1947); also note United States v. Marshall, 526 F2d 1349 (9th Cir., 1976), cert den 426 US 923 (1976).

78. Unreported (4th Cir., January 12, 1988).

79. See also Palmieri v. New York, 779 F2d 861 (2d Cir., 1985).

80. See Oppenheimer Fund, Inc. v. Sanders, 437 US 340 (1978).
81. Supra note 43.
82. See Re Baum, 606 F2d 592 (5th Cir., 1979).
83. Supra note 5 at 210–211.
84. See Lapenna v. Upjohn Company, 110 FRD 15 (ED Pa., 186).
85. Rule 33(b) of FRCP
86. See Harrison v. Prather, 404 F2d 267 (5th Cir., 1968).
87. See Case & Comment (July–August 1987) at 32; also see Weddington v. Consolidated Rail Co., 101 FRD 71 (ND Ind., 1984).
88. "Any party may serve on any other party a request (1) to produce and permit the party making the request, or someone acting on his behalf, to inspect and copy, any designated documents (including writings, drawings, graphs, charts, photographs, phono-records, and other data compilations from which information can be obtained, translated, if necessary, by the respondent through detection devices into reasonably usable form), or to inspect and copy, test, or sample any tangible things which constitute or contain matters within the scope of Rule 26(b) and which are in the possession, custody or control of the party upon whom the request is served; or (2) to permit entry upon designated land or other property in the possession or control of the party upon whom the request is served for the purpose of inspection and measuring, surveying, photographing, testing, or sampling the property or any designated object or operation thereon, within the scope of Rule 26(b)."

Note Standard Dyeing and Finishing Co. v. Arma Textile Printers Corp., unreported (SDNY, 1986), wherein the court rejected the suggestion that the party had fulfilled its obligations under Rule 34(b) of responding to the production of documents by notifying plaintiffs that they should contact a third party and make arrangements to look through a mass of uncategorized paper documents: "It is not sufficient for Hudson to point to a haystack of documents and tell plaintiffs to arrange with Arma for permission to find the needles. Even if Hudson does not have possession of the documents, it has clearly access to them and has the legal right to obtain them. As such Hudson is responsible for producing them in compliance with Rule 34." Thus, the defendant must either produce the documents as they are kept in the usual course of business, or organize and label them to correspond with the categories in the document request: "where as here the state of the corporation's records would make it unreasonably burdensome for the discovering party to search for the sought-after documents, the burden falls on the discoveree to organize the documents so that the discoveror may make 'reasonable use' of them. . . . If Hudson has failed to maintain its records in a reasonable state, it must bear the burden of searching those available records for documents responsive to plaintiffs Rule 34(b) request."

In Gould, Inc. v. Mitsui Mining & Smelting Co., 825 F2d 676 (2d Cir.,

August 3, 1987) the Second U.S. Court of Appeals refused to halt production of documents on the ground that the deposition had been "closed."

89. "When the mental or physical condition (including the blood group) of a party, or of a person in the custody or under the legal control of a party, is in controversy, the court in which the action is pending may order the party to submit to a physical or mental examination by a physician or to produce for examination the person in his custody or legal control. The order may be made only on motion for good cause shown and upon notice to the person to be examined and to all parties and shall specify the time, place, manner, conditions, and scope of the examination and the person or persons by whom it is to be made."

Also see Postell v. Amana Refrigeration, Inc. 87 FRD 706 (ND Ga., 1980).

90. Supra note 87 at 30.

91. See 71 Geo L J 917 (1983), and note Boring v. Keller, 97 FRD 404 (Colo., 1983).

92. See Gardner v. Borden, Inc., 110 FRD 696 (SD W Va., 1986), dismd 812 F2d 1400 (4th Cir., 1987).

93. 639 F Supp 532 (SDNY June 24, 1987).

94. According to the court, "[i]f the jury is to award attorneys fees, then the fee arrangement should be discoverable under the general theory that discovery on any theory of damages is appropriate. If not, then Weisman has advanced no theory under which they would be 'relevant to the subject matter involved in the pending action,' Fed. R. Civ. P. 26(b)(1), and therefore they would not be discoverable."

95. See generally Raleigh, "Attorney-Client Privileges: Implementing Safeguards to Protect Them," Trial Magazine (May 1988) at 45 et seq.

96. See Hickman v. Taylor, 329 US 495 (1947) at 511.

97. Supra note 2 at 159 et seq.

98. 28 USC 1292(b).

99. Cf. Sibbach v. Wilson, 312 US 1 (1941).

100. See generally 15 Mich J L Ref 465 (1982).

101. Note, for example, Mo R Crim P Section 25.03(A)(5). The state of Maryland has a rule of discovery which required the state in a criminal prosecution to disclose to the criminal defendant, even without a request, the acquisition of statements made by the defendant, and, upon request by defendant, to furnish to the defendant all statements made by defendant to a state agent which the state intended to use at the hearing or trial. In Jennings v. State of Maryland, 303 Md 72, 57 ALR4th 813 (1987), the Maryland Court of Appeals affirmed a conviction despite the fact that an undercover police officer was permitted to describe his conversation with the criminal defendant negotiating the purchase of drugs. The court ruled that the term "statements," as used in the Maryland rule of discovery, did not embrace utterances by the accused in the very act of committing the crime! Recordings of conversations

with the defendant during the course of the commission of a crime are ordinarily discoverable as "recordings," not as "statements."

102. See, for example, Ore Rev Stat Section 135.815(3).

103. Note Mass R Crim P Section 14(a) (2).

104. See Chapter 2.

105. 484 NE2d 999 (Mass., 1985).

106. State of Nebraska v. Meis, 351 NW2d 79 (Neb., 1984).

107. 477 So2d 17 (Fla., 1985); here the court explained: "Under Fla. R. Crim. P. 3.220(a)(1), the prosecutor was obligated to disclose the existence of the tape recording at issue and make it available to defendant upon request. The prosecutor attempted to comply with that request but by inadvertently playing the tape at the wrong speed, failed to do so and based upon the mistaken conclusion that the tape was unintelligible, agreed that it would not be used at trial. . . . The state, by agreeing that the tape was unintelligible and unusable, created a situation which was the practical equivalent of never having disclosed the existence of the tape. Consequently, the last minute revelation that the tape was intelligible and usable was as suppressing and potentially prejudicial as if it were the first disclosure of the tape's existence. When it was discovered on the day of the trial that the statement did exist (was intelligible), it is clear that a discovery violation, though unintentional, had occurred."

108. Unreported (January 28, 1988).

109. See National Law Journal (February 8, 1988) at 5.

110. See New York Law Journal (November 3, 1987) at 1 et seq.

111. See Hayes v. County of Nassau, 127 AD2d 742 (2d Dept., 1987) and Ventura v. Long Island Jewish-Hillside Medical Center, 112 AD2d 437 (2d Dept., 1985).

112. Avnet, Inc. v. American Motorists Insurance Co., F Supp (SDNY, May 12, 1987).

113. Unreported (Civil Ct., N.Y. County, January 28, 1988).

114. See generally Trial Magazine (August 1987) at 39 et seq.

115. "A party may in his notice and in a subpoena name as the deponent a public or private corporation or a partnership or association or governmental agency and describe with reasonable particularity the matter on which examination is requested. In that event, the organization so named shall designate one or more officers, directors, or managing agents, or other persons who consent to testify on its behalf, and may set forth, for each person designated, the matters on which he will testify. A subpoena shall advise a non-party organization of its duty to make such a designation. The persons so designated shall testify as to matters known or reasonably available to the organization. This subdivision (b)(6) does not preclude taking a deposition by any other procedure authorized in these rules."

116. Note Cleveland v. Palmby, 75 FRD 654 (WD Okla., 1977).

117. 480 F2d 620 (5th Cir., 1973).

118. 34 Fed R Serv2d 855 (N.J., 1982).

119. See Mitsui Co (USA) Inc. v. Puerto Rico Water Resources Authority, 93 FRD 62 (P.R., 1981) and 687 F2d 501 (1st Cir., 1982), where the notices to the corporation were deemed proper and the corporation had the duty to produce knowledgeable witnesses: "The notices served on defendant comply with the reasonable particularity requirements of Rule 30(b)(6). The notices are sufficient to inform [defendant corporation] of the matters which will be inquired into at the depositions so that [defendant] can determine the identity and number of persons whose presence will be necessary to provide an adequate response to any . . . potential questions. The notice alone is enough to compel the corporation to comply. It is the duty of the corporation to name and produce one or more persons who consent to testify on its behalf as to matters known or reasonably available to the organization [citation omitted]. The burden is on the corporation to decide who will appear for it."

120. Supra notes 110–112.

121. Unreported (New York County, February 1, 1988).

122. See generally For the Defense (October 1987) at 12 et seq.

123. Note the following: Frey v. Chrysler Corp., 41 FRD 174 (WD Pa., 1966); Prashker v. Beech Aircraft Corp., 258 F2d 602 (3d Cir., 1958); Peterson v. Auto Wash Mfg. & Supply Co., 676 F2d 949 (8th Cir., 1982); and Hoppe v. Midwest Conveyor Co., 485 F2d 1196 (8th Cir., 1973).

124. 411 NYS2d 722 (1978).

125. 101 FRD 21 (Minn., 1984) and 747 F2d 1180 (8th Cir., 1984).

126. Unreported (2d Dept., December 15, 1987).

127. See Warren Freedman, The Right of Privacy in the Computer Age (1987).

128. 219 A2d 277 (N.H., 1966).

129. The author was the lead counsel in defending this case.

130. 95 FRD 101 (SD Ohio, 1982).

131. See Uitts v. General Motors Corp., 411 F Supp 1380 (ED Pa., 1974).

132. See Nubbe v. Hardy Continental Hotel System, 31 NW2d 332 (Minn., 1948).

133. See Birmingham Union Railway Co. v. Alexander, 9 So 525 (La., 1891).

134. 639 F Supp 532 (SDNY, September 10, 1987).

135. Unreported (EDNY, 1986), aff (2d Cir., 1987), cert den (1987).

136. See New York Times (November 17, 1987) at A21.

137. Dkt C579863 (1987).

138. See National Law Journal (March 28, 1988) at 3 and 46.

139. 785 F2d 1108 (3d Cir., 1986).

140. See Hartford Courant (February 7, 1988) at Cll. The defendant had apparently spent $14 million to develop a palladium and magnesium nitrate

additive that neutralizes cigarette tar and reduced the incidence of tumor on mouse skin. Furthermore—"A 1961 memorandum from Arthur D. Little Inc.—a Cambridge, Mass., consulting company that began conducting cancer experiments for Liggett in 1954—said: 'There are biologically active materials present in cigarette tobacco. These are: a) cancer causing; b) cancer promoting; c) poisonous. . . .'

The memorandum, titled 'L&M—a Perspective Review' and labeled 'confidential,' appeared to contradict longstanding claims from Liggett and other companies that evidence linking smoking to cancer is inconclusive."

In a 21-page 1961 memorandum, Philip Morris research director Helmut Wakeham noted that developing a "medically acceptable cigarette" would require "reduction of the general level of carcinogenic substances in smoke" and would cost $10 million.

141. According to the court, "As embarrassment is usually thought of as a nonmonetizable harm to individuals, it may be especially difficult for a business enterprise, whose primary measure of well-being is presumably monetizable, to argue for a protective order on this ground [citation omitted]; to succeed, a business will have to show with some specificity that the embarrassment resulting from dissemination of the information would cause a significant harm to its competitive and financial position." Note generally 69 Cornell L Rev 1 (1983).

142. See Zenith Radio Corp. v. Matsushita Electrical Industry Co., 529 F Supp 866 (ED Pa., 1981).

143. See Ledge Hill Farms, Inc. v. W. R. Grace & Co., Inc., 6 Fed R Serv2d 715 (SDNY, 1962).

144. 635 F2d 1295 (7th Cir., 1980).

145. Note Lambert v. Soltis, 221 A2d 173 (Pa., 1966), a dental malpractice case, in which the court affirmed a judgment for a nonsuit because plaintiff presented no expert testimony!

146. "Discovery of facts known and opinion held by experts, otherwise discoverable under the provisions of subdivision (b)(1) of this rule and acquired or developed in anticipation of litigation or trial, may be obtained only as follows:

(A)(i) A party may through interrogatories require any other party to identify each person whom the other party expects to call as an expert witness at trial, to state the subject matter on which the expert is expected to testify and a summary of the grounds for each opinion. (ii) Upon motion, the court may order further discovery by other means. . . .

(B) A party may discover facts known or opinions held by an expert who has been retained or specially employed by another party in anticipation of litigation or preparation for trial and who is not expected to be called as a witness at trial, only as provided in Rule 35(b) (concerning opinion of examining physicians) or upon a showing of exceptional circumstances. . . .

(C) Unless manifest injustice would result, (i) the court shall require that the party seeking discovery pay the expert a reasonable fee . . . and (ii) . . . pay the other party a fair portion of the fees and expenses reasonably incurred by the latter party in obtaining facts and opinions from the expert.''

147. *Rule 702. Testimony by Experts.* If scientific, technical, or other specialized knowledge will assist the trier of fact to understand the evidence or to determine a fact in issue, a witness qualified as an expert by knowledge, skill, experience, training, or education, may testify thereto in the form of an opinion or otherwise.

Rule 703. Bases of Opinion Testimony by Experts. The facts or data in the particular case upon which an expert bases an opinion or inference may be those perceived by or made known to him at or before the hearing. If of a type reasonably relied upon by experts in the particular field in forming opinions or inferences upon the subject, the facts or data need not be admissible in evidence.

Rule 704. Opinion on Ultimate Issue. Testimony in the form of an opinion or inference otherwise admissible is not objectionable because it embraces an ultimate issue to be decided by the trier of fact.

Rule 705. Disclosure of Facts or Data Underlying Expert Opinion. The expert may testify in terms of opinion or inference and give his reasons therefor without prior disclosure of the underlying facts or data, unless the court requires otherwise. The expert may in any event be required to disclose the underlying facts or data on cross-examination.''

148. See Roberts v. United States, 316 F2d 489 (3d Cir., 1963).

149. Note Frey v. United States, 293 Fed 1013 (D.C., 1923).

150. See Chapter 2, and note ABA Code of Professional Responsibility, Canon 7, Sections 7-28, D R 7-109(c)(3).

151. See For the Defense (July 1987) at 16.

152. 640 F Supp 155 (SDNY, December 4, 1987).

153. See Knowles & Vote, ''Limiting Descovery Through Protective Orders,'' For the Defense (January 1987) at 18 et seq.

154. Note Farnsworth v. Procter & Gamble Co., 758 F2d 1545 (11th Cir., 1985).

155. 138 F Supp (SDNY, 1956).

156. 89 FRD (ND Cal., 1981).

157. Note Sherman & Kinnard, Federal Court Discovery in the 80s—Making the Rules Work, 95 FRD 245 (1983).

158. 724 F2d 1010 (DC Cir., 1984).

159. Id.

160. 467 US 20 (1984).

161. Note that Rule 26(c) of FRCP does not specifically refer to privacy or to other rights and interests that may be implicated because ''such matters are implicit in the broad purpose and language of the Rule.''

162. Unreported (SDNY, December 1, 1987).

163. 779 F2d 861 (2d Cir., 1985).

164. Id. at 866.

165. See Rule 26(b)(4)(B) of FRCP.

166. 662 F2d 496 (10th Cir., 1980).

167. See Bailey v. Meister Brau, Inc., 57 FRD 11 (ND Ill., 1972).

168. See, for example, Pearl Brewing Co. v. Joseph Schlitz Brewing Co., 415 F Supp 1122 (SD Texas, 1976).

169. 828 F2d (2d Cir., September 10, 1987).

170. According to the federal appellate court, "The district court made several relevant rulings, holding initially that the petitioner waived his attorney-client privilege by acquiescing in and encouraging the publication of *Reversal of Fortune*. It then examined the scope of the waiver. In so doing the district judge found that the waiver extended to (1) the contents of the published conversations, (2) all communications between petitioner and attorney Dershowitz relating to the published conversations, and (3) all communications between petitioner and any defense counsel relating to the published conversations. We examine each of these rulings.

A. *The Waiver of the Attorney-Client Privilege*

By allowing publication of confidential communications in his attorney's book *Reversal of Fortune*, petitioner was held to have waived his attorney-client privilege. In reaching that conclusion, the district court considered the following facts. First, petitioner knew of, consented to, and actually encouraged attorney Dershowitz's plans to write a book providing an "insider look" into his case. Second, petitioner was warned before publication that such an act might trigger a waiver and, yet, took no active measures to preserve his confidences. Third, after publication, petitioner joined his attorney in enthusiastically promoting the book on television and radio shows. Based on these key facts, the district court determined that von Bulow had waived his attorney-client privilege.

Petitioner argues that this holding is erroneous because only the client—and not his attorney—may waive the privilege. Of course, the privilege belongs solely to the client and may only be waived by him. An attorney may not waive the privilege without his client's consent. *Republic Gear Co. v. Borg-Warner Corp.*, 381 F.2d 551, 556 (2d Cir. 1967). Hence, absent a client's consent or waiver, the publication of confidential communications by an attorney does not constitute a relinquishment of the privilege by the client. *See, e.g., Schnell v. Schnell*, 550 F.Supp. 650, 653 (SDNY 1982) (no waiver of attorney-client privilege where attorney testified at SEC hearing without presence or authorization of client). *See also Wigmore, supra*, §2325, 633 (attorney's voluntary disclosures remain privileged unless impliedly authorized by client).

A client may nonetheless by his actions impliedly waive the privilege or consent to disclosure. . . .

Applying these principles, it is quite clear that in finding that von Bulow waived his privilege the district court did not abuse its discretion. In light of petitioner's acquiescence in and encouragement of *Reversal of Fortune's* publication, Judge Walker properly concluded that von Bulow consented to his attorney's disclosure of his confidences and effectively waived his attorney-client privilege. Our discussion now turns to examine the breadth of that waiver.

B. *The Scope of the Waiver*

1. *The Contents of the Published Conversations*

The district court held that plaintiffs were entitled to discover "the entire contents of all conversations from which Dershowitz published extracts in *Reversal of Fortune.*" 114 FRD at 79. The four relevant conversations between von Bulow and his attorneys were their initial one, and the ones regarding the bail hearing, appellate strategy, and von Bulow's decision to testify on his own behalf. Id. at 79 n.2. Under that ruling, plaintiff is permitted to discover those parts of the four identified conversations not made public in the book. Petitioner argues that the district court's holding improperly broadened the fairness doctrine to include extrajudicial disclosures and that, accordingly, the discovery order cannot stand. We agree. . . .

These considerations—which underlie "the fairness doctrine"—aim to prevent prejudice to a party and distortion of the judicial process that may be caused by the privilege-holder's selective disclosure during litigation of otherwise privileged information. Under the doctrine the client alone controls the privilege and may or may not choose to divulge his own secrets. But it has been established law for a hundred years that when the client waives the privilege by testifying about what transpired between her and her attorney, she cannot thereafter insist that the mouth of the attorney be shut. *Hunt v. Blackburn,* 128 US 464, 470–71 (1888). From that has grown the rule that testimony as to part of a privileged communication, in fairness, requires production of the remainder. *McCormick On Evidence* §93, at 194–95 (2d ed. 1972).

Yet this rule protecting the party, the factfinder, and the judicial process from selectively disclosed and potentially misleading evidence does not come into play when, as here, the privilege-holder or his attorney has made extrajudicial disclosures, and those disclosures have not subsequently been placed at issue during litigation. In fact, the cases finding, as the district court did here, implied waivers on account of fairness involved material issues raised by a client's assertions during the course of a judicial proceeding. . . .

Applying the fairness doctrine, we hold therefore that the extrajudicial disclosure of an attorney-client communication—one not subsequently used by the client in a judicial proceeding to his adversary's prejudice—does not waive the privilege as to the undisclosed portions of the communication. Hence, though the district court correctly found a waiver by von Bulow as to the particular matters *actually disclosed* in the book, it was an abuse of discretion to broaden that waiver to include those portions of the four identified conversations which, because they were not published, remain secret. . . .

But where, as here, disclosures of privileged information are made extrajudicially and without prejudice to the opposing party, there exists no reason in logic or equity to broaden the waiver beyond those matters actually revealed. Matters actually disclosed in public lose their privileged status because they obviously are no longer confidential. The cat is let out of the bag, so to speak. But related matters not so disclosed remain confidential. Although it is true that disclosures in the public arena may be "one-sided" or "misleading," so long as such disclosures are and remain extrajudicial, there is no *legal* prejudice that warrants a broad court-imposed subject matter waiver. The reason is that disclosures made in public rather than in court—even if selective—create no risk of *legal* prejudice until put at issue in the litigation by the privilege-holder. Therefore, insofar as the district court broadened petitioner's waiver to include related conversations on the same subject it was in error. . . .

2. *Related Conversation With Dershowitz*

The district court next ruled that von Bulow's waiver extended to subject matter areas related to the published conversations with Dershowitz. 114 FRD at 79. This "subject matter waiver," which allows the attacking party to reach all privileged conversations regarding a particular subject once one privileged conversation on that topic has been disclosed, is simply another form of the waiver by implication rule discussed above. Like the "implied waiver," the subject matter waiver also rests on the fairness considerations at work in the context of litigation. See *Smith,* 538 F. Supp. at 979 ("It would be unfair to allow a client to assert the attorney-client privilege and prevent disclosure of damaging communications while allowing the client to disclose other selected communications solely for self-serving purposes").

For this reason, it too has been invoked most often where the privilege-holder has attempted to use the privilege as both "a sword" and "a shield" or where the attacking party has been prejudiced at trial. *See In Re Sealed Case,* 676 F.2d 793, 809 n.54 (D.C.Cir., 1982) (Courts retain discretion "not to impose full waiver as to all communications on the same subject matter where the client has merely disclosed a communication to a third party, as opposed to making some use of it.") . . .

3. *Related Conversations with Other Defense Attorneys*

Again invoking the fairness doctrine, the district court found that von Bulow's waiver extended to his conversations with all other defense attorneys which relate to the subject matter disclosed in the book. 114 FRD at 80. Since we have already found that the publication of *Reversal of Fortune* did not result in a sweeping subject matter waiver, that waiver *a fortiori* cannot extend to von Bulow's other attorneys."

171. See generally 94 Harv L Rev 1085 (1981).

172. 785 F2d 1108 (3d Cir., 1986); also supra note 139.

173. Note the admonition in Rule 1 of FRCP that there must be "just, speedy, and inexpensive determination of every action."

174. 594 F2d 594 (7th Cir., 1978), cert den 440 US 971 (1979).

175. Unreported (SDNY, May 1, 1987).

176. 794 F2d 64 (2d Cir., September 16, 1987).

177. See Warren Freedman, Press and Media Access to the Criminal Courtroom (1988).

178. See The Brief (Winter 1988) at 52.

179. 598 F2d 176 (DC Cir., 1979).

180. Supra note 171 at 1089.

181. See Martindell v. International Telephone & Telegraph Corp., 594 F2d 291 (2d Cir., 1979).

182. Supra note 174.

183. 332 F2d 260 (9th Cir., 1963), cert den 379 US 900 (1964).

184. Supra note 171 at 1093.

185. 410 F2d 553 (5th Cir., 1969), cert den 396 US 820 (1969).

186. Supra note 171 at 1094.

187. See Warren Freedman, International Products Liability (2 vol., 1987) at § 9.09

188. See Patterson v. Ford Motor Co., 85 FRD 152 (WD Tex., 1980) at 154, and Williams v. Johnson & Johnson, 50 FRD 31 (SDNY, 1970).

189. 415 F Supp 129 (SDNY, 1976).

190. Id. at 132; also supra note 171 at 1098. Subsequently Congress enacted the Hart-Scott-Rodino Antitrust Improvements Act of 1976 (Publ L 94-435, 90 Stat 1383) which empowered the Department of Justice to do just that!

191. 397 US 1 (1970).

192. See Warren Freedman and Edward Greer, Litigation: Toxic Torts (1989) at Section 4.5.

193. See Priest v. Rotary, 98 FRD 755 (ND Cal., 1983), setting forth a series of detailed questions on prior sexual partners and activities of a plaintiff female alleging sexual harassment in the workplace.

194. Note Campbell v. U.S. Dept. of Agriculture, 515 F Supp 1239 (DC., 1981) at 1245.

195. See generally 20 Internat Lawyer (Spring 1986) at 502.

196. See, for example, United States Arbitration Act, 9 USC 1 et seq. (1925); also supra note 187 at Chapter 19.

197. See, for example, the Uniform Arbitration Act (1955).

198. See Goldstein, A Lawyer's Guide to Arbitration (1977) at 41.

199. Supra note 196.

200. 371 F Supp 240 (EDNY, 1973).

201. Id. at 246.

202. Supra note 196.
203. See 9 USC 7.
204. Supra note 197.
205. See AAA Rule 10.
206. Supra note 195 at 504 et seq.
207. 135 NJ Super 552 (1975); but the appellate court remanded after finding nothing in the record to show that the party intentionally withheld documents.
208. See, for example, NLRB v. Custom Excavating, Inc., 575 F2d 102 (7th Cir., 1978).
209. 385 US 432 (1967).
210. Id. at 435.
211. See Local Lodge 1746 of International Association of Machinists v. Pratt & Whitney Division of United Aircraft Corp., 329 F Supp 283 (Conn., 1971).
212. See New York Law Journal (September 2, 1987) at 1 et seq.
213. 11 USC 362 (1987).
214. 40 Bankr 219 (SDNY, 1984).
215. See Warren Freedman, Hazardous Waste Liability (1987) at Chapter 12. Also see A. H. Robins Co. v. Piccinin, 788 F2d 994 (4th Cir., 1985), cert den 107 S Ct 251 (1986).
216. 26 Bankr 420 (Bankr SDNY, 1983) at 425 and 426.
217. 540 F2d 755 (4th Cir., 1976).
218. 39 Bankr 659 (SDNY, 1984).
219. Id. at 661.
220. 373 F Supp 191 (SDNY, 1974).
221. In First & Merchants National Bank v. Bailey, 11 Bankr 199 (ED Va., 1981) the plaintiff sought relief from the stay to take discovery of the defendant-debtor to defend itself against the debtor's counterclaim, arguing that the limited discovery was not the type of interference with the bankruptcy contemplated by the Bankruptcy Code, and the court agreed: "[A]ny other decision to the contrary would be clearly inequitable, for it would allow the defendant to pursue a claim against the plaintiff without giving the plaintiff the opportunity to defend itself. Further, this court does not see any interference to the defendant in his bankruptcy proceeding for it is the defendant himself who is pursuing an action against the plaintiff and hence, any alleged interference in the bankruptcy case is by the defendant's own doing."
222. See 16 NYU Internat Law & Pol 985 (1985).
223. See Freedman, International Products Liability at Chapter 9.
224. See the following section in this chapter.
225. Supra note 223 at 416–417.
226. See 2 Review of Litigation 119–154 (1981–82).
227. Supra note 222 at 985.
228. See first Reporters' Note to Section 420 in Tentative Draft No. 3 of

the Restatement of the Foreign Relations Law of the United States; supra note 227.

229. Supra note 222 at 959.

230. 691 F2d 1384 (11th Cir., 1982), cert den 103 S Ct 3086 (1983).

231. 699 F2d 341 (7th Cir., 1983).

232. See the last section of this chapter.

233. 529 F Supp 866 (ED Pa., 1981).

234. Supra note 223 at Chapter 12.

235. 709 F2d 585 (9th Cir., 1983). Here in an antitrust proceeding the nonparty Japanese company had previously charged the defendants with payment of illegal rebates, and the defendants here asserted by way of affirmative defenses and counterclaims that the Japanese company had also paid rebates in the same trade. To support its allegations against the Japanese company defendants requested the production of documents relating to such rebates in the possession, custody, or control of plaintiff's agents, and the federal district court ordered the Japanese company to produce the documents: "The documents so obtained proved the existence of rebates, although plaintiff contended that the discovery order . . . was improper and overbroad."

236. Unreported (June 16, 1987).

237. See generally 33 Torts & Ins L J (Fall 1987) at 70. Also note 62 Yale L J 51 (1953).

238. Supra note 223 at 422–423.

239. 549 F2d 597 (9th Cir., 1976).

240. According to the court, "The elements to be weighed include the degree of conflict with foreign law or policy, the nationality or allegiance of the parties and the locations or principal places of business of corporations, the extent to which enforcement by either state can be expected to achieve compliance, the relative significance of the effects on the United States as compared with those elsewhere, the extent to which there is explicit purpose to harm or affect American commerce, the foreseeability of such effect, and the relative importance to the violations charged of conduct within the United States as compared with conduct abroad."

241. See 4 Fordham L Rev 244 (1935) and Schlesinger, Comparative Law (4th ed., 1980) at 398.

242. Supra note 237 at 72–73.

243. Note that this procedure coincides with the procedure permitted by Article 5(a) of the Hague Service Convention, delineated in the third section of this chapter.

244. Supra note 223 at § 9.10.

245. Note The Signe, 37 F Supp 819 (ED La., 1941): "Letters rogatory are the medium, in effect, whereby one country, speaking through one of its courts, requests another country, acting through its own courts, and by methods of court procedure peculiar thereto and entirely within the latter's control, to assist the administration of justice in the former country; such request being

made, and being usually granted, by reason of the comity existing between nations in ordinary peaceful times.''

246. See International Controls Corp. v. Vesco, 593 F2d 166 (2d Cir., 1978), cert den 442 US 941 (1979).

247. Note 9 Internat Law 717 (1975).

248. See, for example, Federal Trade Commission v. Compagnie de Saint-Gobain-Pont-a-Mousson, 493 F Supp 286 (DC, 1980), vac 636 F2d 1300 (DC Cir., 1980).

249. Supra note 242 at 85.

250. See United States v. Paraffin Wax Co., 23 FRD 289 (SDNY, 1959).

251. See Epstein, ''English Discovery: Simpler and Cheaper,'' National Law Journal (November 28, 1988) at 17–19.

252. Restatement of Foreign Relations Law of the United States (Revised § 420, Tentative Draft No. 3 [1982]).

253. Note Section 420 on Jurisdiction.

254. Id. at Section 420(1)(a).

255. Note that Rule 26 of FRCP was amended on August 1, 1983 to limit discovery requests: the trial court, upon its own initiative, may limit discovery because (i) it is duplicative or unnecessary, (ii) some other source of information is more convenient, (iii) the party seeking discovery has already had ample opportunity to obtain the information sought, or (iv) the discovery sought is unduly burdensome, given the structure of the case and the limits on the parties' resources. Subsection (g) mandates that attorneys sign all discovery papers.

256. Note Section 419 on foreign government compulsion.

257. Section 419, Comment b.

258. Supra note 222 at 1077.

259. 357 US 197 (1958).

260. Supra note 222 at 1082–1083.

261. See Atwood & Brewster, Antitrust and American Business Abroad (2d ed., 1981) and 83 Columbia L Rev 1320 (1983).

262. 20 UST 361, T.I.A.S. No. 6638, 658 USTS 163.

263. Supra note 223 at § 11.14.

264. See Tamari v. Bache & Co. (Lebanon), S.A., 431 F Supp 1266 (ND Ill., 1976), aff 565 F2nd 1194 (7th Cir., 1977), cert den 435 US 905 (1978).

265. 28 USC 1330 et seq. (1977).

266. Unreported (Oct. 3, 1984).

267. According to the court, the convention ''provides for the service of judicial documents abroad. Its preeminent provision, and the vehicle by which control of service of process is insured, is the creation of a central authority to be designated by each signatory nation to the treaty (ch. 1, art. 2). This central authority has the responsibility for receiving the requests for service, serving the judicial documents and certifying and returning the certificates of

service (ch. 1, arts. 3–6). The prescribed method of service is outlined in Article 5 of the Convention. Japan has objected to the service by mailing provision in The Hague Convention (Article 10). Plaintiff must, therefore, follow the procedure in Article 5. Not only has the plaintiff not done so, plaintiff argues that the Hague Convention is inapplicable. This argument is without merit. Plaintiff has not demonstrated that defendant Nissan, Ltd. is amenable to any other form of process.''

268. 506 NYS2d 393 (1986).

269. See Shoei Kako Co. v. Superior Court, 198 Cal Rptr 402 (1973).

270. Supra note 222 at 76.

271. Supra note 265 at Article 4.

272. See generally 36 Baylor L Rev 131 (1984) and 34 Sw L J 1013 (1982).

273. 597 F Supp 1082 (ED Va., 1984).

274. 697 F2d 574 (4th Cir., 1983).

275. See DeJames v. Magnificence Carriers, Inc. 654 F2d 280 (3d Cir., 1981), where the court observed, ''We believe that the purpose and nature of the treaty demonstrate that it does not provide independent authorization for service of process in a foreign country. The treaty merely provides a mechanism by which a plantiff authorized to serve process under the laws of the country can effect service that will give appropriate notice to the party being served and will not be objectionable to the country in which that party is served.

We find further support for this conclusion in the fact that the treaty applies to parties desiring to make service in state-court proceedings. The nature of the judicial system of the United States, which includes not only the federal courts but also the many state systems with their differing procedural requirements, was one of the primary justifications for entering into a treaty that would provide a uniform, valid method of effecting service. . . .

We do not believe that the treaty in any way affects a state's chosen limits on the jurisdictional reach of its courts. If a state long-arm rule does not authorize service outside the United States, a litigant in the state would have no authority to invoke the methods of serving process provided by the treaty. We believe that the treaty merely serves as an important adjunct to state long-arm rules, and that it specifies a valid method of effecting service only if the state long-arm rule authorizes service abroad.

Further, we believe that the same principle applies to the use of the treaty in conjunction with the Federal Rules of Civil Procedure. . . .

Therefore, in order for DeJames to validly serve process on Hitachi in Japan, there must not only be a method of effecting such service but also a state or federal statute authorizing service abroad.'' (pp. 288–290)

276. See Harris v. Browning-Ferris Industries Chemical Services, Inc., 100 FRD 775 (MD La., 1984) where the court observed that Rule 4(i) of FRCP is ''intended to cover those instances where service in a foreign country is not prohibited by an international treaty.''

277. T.I.A.S. No. 10, 072, 20 ILM 1405 (1981).

278. See T.I.A.S. No. 10072 on abolishing the requirement of legislation for foreign public documents.

279. 23 UST 2555, T.I.A.S. No. 7444, 8 ILM 37 (1969).

280. Supra note 223 at 423–424.

281. The New York Law Journal (September 25, 1984) at 4 analyzed these five articles as follows:

	Article 15 (Nationals)	Article 16 (Consulate)	Article 17 (Commissi- oners)	Article 18 (Compulsion)	Article 23 (Pre-Trial)
Barbados	Y	P	P	N	Y
Cyprus	Y	P	P	N	Y
Czechoslovakia	Y	w/o P[1]	w/o P[1]	Y	Y
Denmark	P	P	N	N	N
Finland	Y	w/o P	w/o P	N	N
France	Y	P w/c	P w/c	N	N
Germany (West)	Y	P[2]	P w/c	N	N
Israel	Y	P	P	N	Y
Italy	Y	P	P	Y	N
Luxembourg	Y	P w/c	P w/c	N	N
Netherlands	Y	w/o P	P w/c	N	N
Norway	P	P	P	N	N
Portugal	P	N	N	N	N
Singapore	N	N	N	N	N
Sweden	P	P	P	N	N
U.K.	Y	w/o P[1]	w/o P	Y	N
U.S.A.	Y	w/o P	w/o P	Y	Y

w/o P = No permission required

P = Permission required

P w/c = Permission required, conditions specified

Y = Yes (available upon request)

N = Not (not available)

(1) On the condition reciprocity is applied.

(2) Applies only to nationals of third states - no permission required for German nationals or nationals of requesting jurisdiction.

282. Supra note 223 at 506, ftn. 104.

283. See United States v. Pink, 315 US 203 (1942).

284. Unreported (Conn., 1982).

285. 100 FRD 58 (ED Pa., 1983).

286. Française D'Assurance Pour Le Commerce Extérieur v. Phillips Petroleum Co., 105 FRD 16 (SDNY, 1984).

287. 754 F2d 602 (5th Cir., 1985). Note the Brief for the United States as amicus curiae, filed on March 24, 1986 (at 24 ILM 804 et seq.).

288. 107 S Ct 2542 (1987). See Feldman, "Foreign Discovery: A New Complication", Trial Magazine (March, 1988) at 67, where the author observed, "Plaintiffs can no longer expect federal district courts routinely to order foreign discovery under the Federal Rules of Civil Procedure. Instead, the trial judge may, in the interest of comity and after balancing all the interests, order that the plaintiff first try to obtain discovery through the foreign court where the evidence is located by using procedures of the Evidence Convention. This determination is to be made case by case after a "particularized" analysis of all the facts and interests.

As a consequence of the Supreme Court ruling in *Société Nationale Industrielle Aerospatiale v. United States District Court for the Southern District of Iowa,* all discovery in Convention countries will be conducted under the supervision of U.S. or foreign courts and is likely to be more limited than the broad pretrial discovery conducted under the Federal Rules. Trial lawyers who want to avoid foreign courts or to exploit foreign procedures effectively must be familiar with international judicial assistance and with the rules of civil procedure of the foreign country. A crucial issue in every proceeding under *Aerospatiale* will be the prospect for reasonable, timely discovery abroad. Procedures in some countries, e.g. the Federal Republic of Germany, are in flux, and it will take time to determine whether discovery under the Evidence Convention is consistent with the fair administration of justice as mandated by the Federal Rules."

In the first case after the U.S. Supreme Court's determination, the federal district court for the Northern District of New York in Hudson v. Pfauter, 117 FRD 33 (NDNY, 1987) ordered the plaintiff to serve interrogatories on a West German defendant under the Evidence Convention. The court intimated that the West German authorities must cooperate and that the U.S. court would have the last word on discovery required from the foreign defendant. Subsequently on March 3, 1988 in Haynes v. Kleinewefers, the federal district court for the Eastern District of New York rejected a West German company's efforts to have discovery in a products liability case governed by the Evidence Convention instead of the Federal Rules of Evidence. The court surmised that discovery under the Evidence Convention could delay proceedings by requiring the injured plaintiff to seek discovery under a West German procedure that "can be a very time-consuming and expensive effort." Furthermore, it appeared that the West German concern had agreed "in the alternative" to depositions in the U.S. after a third-party defendant stated that it would absorb the cost of the depositions. The court emphasized that the use of the Evidence Convention procedures was "optional" at the discretion of the trial court. The plaintiff here had sued the defendant manufacturer of a plastic-molding machine as a result of an accident in 1987 that resulted in the amputation of plaintiff's right arm. Plaintiff alleged that his injury was caused by defendant's failure to post guard rails around the machine. See generally New York Law Journal (March 3, 1988) at 32.

289. 788 F2d 1408 (9th Cir., 1986).

290. Note the Tenth U.S. Court of Appeals' decision in the Daimler-Benz Aktiengesellschaft v. U.S. District Court, 805 F2d 340 (10th Cir., 1986), which ruled that the Hague Evidence Convention had no application to the production of evidence in the U.S. by a party who is subject to the jurisdiction of the federal district court.

291. This reading of Article 27 is attested to by the statement of the rapporteur of the commission which drafted the convention: "The Convention contains in Article 27 the same provision as the Documents Convention to *preserve for each signatory party all provisions of its internal law that are more favorable to, and grant more generous assistance to, foreign courts and litigants than the methods prescribed in the Convention.* This gives the foreign court or litigant the better of two possible worlds. If the domestic law of the requested state is more beneficial and more flexible in favor of the foreign litigant than the Convention techniques, those more liberal rules of the domestic law will remain available to the foreign litigant and the requesting authority. . . .

This is a most important article, designed to preserve existing internal law and practice in a Contracting State which provides broader, more general and less restrictive rules of international cooperation in the taking of evidence *for the benefit of foreign courts and litigants.*

It permits in sub-division (a) a declaration authorizing the use of channels of transmission other than the Central Authority, e.g. consular or diplomatic channels or transmission direct 'from court to court,' or by the parties.

It provides, in sub-division (b) that any act provided for in the Convention may be performed upon less restrictive conditions than the Convention provides, if the internal law or practice *of the State of execution so permits.* This will be particularly applicable to Chapter II, with respect to those States which presently give consuls and commissioner substantially unlimited freedom to take the evidence of willing witnesses.

It provides, in sub-division (c), for methods of taking evidence other than those provided in the Convention, to the extent that internal law and practice will permit. This means taking evidence without either a Letter of Request or the use of a consul or commissioner.

For example, counsel for the parties may travel to the home of a willing witness, call in a local official to administer an oath, and then question the witness, making a record by stenographer or tape recorder. Or to save travel expense, competent local counsel in the State of execution could be briefed to examine the witness. *The only conditions are that the State of execution will permit this,* and that the resulting record will be admissible at the trial of the action. If these conditions are met, the result is just as satisfactory as if a Letter of Request had been executed or a consul or commissioner had been appointed to act.

Another example would be for the parties or counsel, with an engineer, to inspect, examine, photograph, measure or test certain machinery in a factory, or the inside of a mine, with the consent of the owner, to obtain evidence for use at the trial of the action. Again, *if the State of execution will permit this,* the result may be completely satisfactory.

A final example is the illustration given in the Report to the draft Convention, where the courts in New York and Chicago appointed foreign German and Italian judges as 'commissioners' and granted compulsion against the witnesses, so that they might examine the witnesses in New York and Chicago in their own language, and under their own procedure, without interference or participation by the local courts. *If the internal law and practice of a particular State offers these broad privileges to foreign courts and litigants,* which go beyond anything provided for in the Convention, that State may safely sign and ratify the Convention without thereby affecting its right to continue to offer these extra benefits to foreign courts and litigants." [Amram, "Explanatory Report of the Convention on the Taking of Evidence Abroad in Civil or Commercial Matters," 12 Int'l Legal Materials 327, 141–42 (1973)].

292. Hague Conference Permanent Bureau Note on the Operation of the Hague Convention of 18 March 1970 on the Taking of Evidence Abroad in Civil or Commercial Matters (Preliminary Doc. No. 1 of March 1985); Report on the Second Meeting of the Special Commission on the Operation of The Hague (Evidence) Convention, prepared by the Permanent Bureau, July 1985; see 24 ILM 1668 (1985).

293. 435 So2d 369 (Fla App, 1983).

294. 117 FRD 16 (Maine, 1987).

295. 20 UST at 363.

296. The court was totally persuaded by the decision in Mommsen v. Toro Company, 108 FRD 444 (SD Iowa, 1985), where the court reasoned as follows: "The provision at issue here, subparagraph (a) of Article 10, does not expressly allow 'service' of judicial process by postal channels in signatory nations; it merely permits one to 'send' judicial documents by mail to persons abroad. It is a 'familiar canon of statutory construction that the starting point for interpreting a statute is the language of the statute itself. Absent a clearly expressed legislative intention to the contrary, that language must ordinarily be regarded as conclusive.' In addition, where a legislative body 'includes

particular language in one section of a statute but omits it in another section of the same Act, it is generally presumed that [the legislative body] acts intentionally and purposely in the disparate inclusion or exclusion.' Finally, where a legislative body 'uses terms that have accumulated meaning under either equity or the common law, a court must infer, unless the statute otherwise dictates, that the [legislative body] means to incorporate the established meaning of those terms.' The Hague Convention repeatedly refers to 'service' of documents, and if the drafters of the Convention had meant for subparagraph (a) of Article 10 to provide an additional manner of service of judicial documents, they would have used the word 'service'; to hold that subparagraph (a) permits direct mail service of process, would go beyond the plain meaning of the word "send" and would create a method of service of process at odds with the other methods of service permitted by the Convention. Sending a copy of a summons and complaint by registered mail directly to a defendant in a foreign country is not a method of service of process allowed by the Hague Convention.

On the general picture of discovery abroad, note the following important references: von Mehren, "Discovery Abroad: The Prospective of the U.S. Private Practititioner," 16 NYU Internat Law & Politics 985 (1984); Struve, "Discovery from Foreign Parties in Civil Cases before U.S. Courts," 16 NYU Internat Law & Politics 1101 (1984); Radvan, "The Hague Convention on Taking of Evidence Abroad in Civil or Commercial Matters: Several Notes Concerning Its Scope, Methods and Compulsion," 16 NYU Internat Law & Politics 1031 (1984); Sadoff, "The Hague Evidence Convention: Problems at Home of Obtaining Foreign Evidence," 20 Internat Lawyer (Spring, 1986) at 659; Olsen, "Discovery in Federal Criminal Investigations," 16 NYU Internat Law & Politics 999 (1984); and note "Extraterritorial Jurisdiction," 16 NYU Internat Law & Politics 1135 (1984).

297. 456 U S 694 (1982). Article 3 of the Hague Evidence Convention requires that the following matters be set forth in the letter of request: "(1) the name and address of the requesting authority and of the authority requested to execute it, if known; (2) the names and addresses of the parties to the proceedings and their representatives, if any; (3) the nature of the proceedings for which the evidence is required, and pertinent information with respect to the particulars thereof; (4) the specific evidence to be obtained, or the other judicial act to be performed; (5) the names and addresses of the persons to be examined; (6) the questions to be put to the persons to be examined, or, alternately, a statement of the underlying facts in sufficient detail to enable the foreign authority to formulate its own questions; (7) a complete description of the documents or other property, real or personal, to be inspected, if applicable; (8) any requirement that the testimony be given on oath or affirmation, and if so, any special form to be used. The language used must be that of the

requesting country or a certified translation must accompany the English letter of request, including a certificate attesting to the accuracy of the translation."

298. Note 16 NYU Internat Law & Pol 1061 (1984).

299. 653 F Supp 957 (SDNY, 1987).

300. See 14 New Eng L Rev 18 (1978) at 56.

301. Société Internationale pour Participations Industrielles et Commerciales, S.A. v. Rogers, 357 US 197 (1958).

302. See Securities & Exchange Commission v. Banca Della Svizzera Italiana, 92 FRD 111 (SDNY, 1981).

303. Foreign Proceedings (Prohibition of Certain Evidence) Act, Australian Acts No. 121 (1976).

304. Uranium Information Security Regulations, Canada Stat 0 & Regs No. 76-644 (1976).

305. French Law No. 538 (1980).

306. Atomic Energy Act No. 90 of 1967 (South Africa).

307. Protection of Trading Interests Act, 1980, ch. 11 (United Kingdom).

308. 549 F2d 597 (9th Cir., 1976): "The elements to be weighed include the degree of conflict with foreign law or policy, the nationality or allegiance of the parties and the locations or principal places of business of corporations, the extent to which enforcement by either state can be expected to achieve compliance, the relative significance of the effects on the United States as compared with those elsewhere, the extent to which there is explicit purpose to harm or affect American commerce, the foreseeability of such effect, and the relative importance to the violations charged of conduct within the United States as compared with conduct abroad. [footnote omitted]" (at 6/4).

309. Note 18 Internat Law 773 (Fall, 1984).

310. See Rules of Procedure of the Inter-American Commercial Arbitration Commission (eff. 1/1/78).

311. The Rules of Procedure of the Inter-American Commercial Arbitration Commission are practically identical with the UNCITRAL rules, but have their own special quality.

312. See 20 Internat Lawyer (Spring, 1986) at 514.

313. Note Cine Forty-Second Street Theatre Corp. v. Allied Artists Pictures Corp., 602 F2d 1062 (2d Cir., 1979) at 1063.

314. See, for example, Torrington Co. v. Metal Products Workers Local 1645, 362 F2d 677 (2d Cir., 1966).

315. AAA Commercial Arbitration Rules, in effect April 1, 1985.

316. Effective September 1, 1984.

317. Rule 13 thereof.

318. Rule 12 thereof.

319. See 26 ILM 1137 (1985).

320. See Ohio Arbitration Act § 2711.07 and Pennsylvania Arbitration Act § 16, delineated in note 223 at 751.

321. Supra note 223 at 180 et seq. (November 1987 Cumulative Supplement).

322. See the 1927 decision of the Permanent Court of International Justice. S.S. Lotus (France v. Turkey), 1927 P.C.I.J., ser A, No. 10 at 18.

323. See The Nereide, 13 US (9 CRanch) 388 (1815).

324. See United States v. First National City Bank, 699 F2d 341 (7th Cir., 1983) and United States v. Vetco, 644 F2d 1324 (9th Cir., 1981), for example.

325. See Consolidated Rendering Co. v. State of Vermont, 207 US 541 (1907).

326. Supra note 222 at 1142 et seq.

327. See, for example, In re Grand Jury Proceedings United States v. Feld, 532 F2d 404 (5th Cir., 1976), cert den 429 US 940 (1976). Interestingly, a civil protective order cannot shield a deposition from a federal grand jury subpoena, according to the Fourth U.S. Court of Appeals in Foremost Guaranty Corp. v. Community Savings & Loan Assn., unreported (4th Cir., 1988). The effect of the ruling means that litigants in civil matters cannot rely on Fifth Amendment protection unless that issue is raised prior to the protective order in the court on the civil matter. A protective order cannot substitute for invoking the privilege against self-incrimination, and it should not be afforded that status. See National Law Journal (February 22, 1988) at 10.

328. Note Arthur Andersen & Co. v. Finesilver, 546 F2d 338 (10th Cir., 1976), cert den 429 US 1096 (1977).

329. 691 F2d 1384 (11th Cir., 1982), cert den 103 S Ct 3086 (1983).

330. Supra note 222 at 999 et seq.

331. Note the fifth section of this chapter.

332. 720 F2d 1327 (DC Cir., 1983).

333. 27 UST 2019, T.I.A.S. No. 8302 (May 25, 1973).

334. 707 F2d 663 (2d Cir., 1983), cert den 103 S Ct 3555 (1983).

335. Id. at 667–668.

336. See the second section of this chapter.

337. "Limitations on Jurisdiction to Prescribe

(1) Although one of the bases for jurisdiction under § 402 is present, a state may not apply law to the conduct, relations, status, or interests of persons or things having connections with another state or states when the exercise of such jurisdiction is unreasonable.

(2) Whether the exercise of jurisdiction is unreasonable is judged by evaluating all the relevant factors, including:

    (a) the extent to which the activity (i) takes place within the regulating state or (ii) has substantial, direct, and foreseeable effect upon or in the regulating state;

(b) the links, such as nationality, residence, or economic activity, between the regulating state and the persons principally responsible for the activity to be regulated, or between that state and those whom the law or regulation is designed to protect;

(c) the character of the activity to be regulated, the importance of regulation to the regulating state, the extent to which other states regulate such activities, and the degree to which the desirability of such regulation is generally accepted;

(d) the existence of justified expectations that might be protected or hurt by the regulation in question;

(e) the importance of regulation to the international political, legal or economic system;

(f) the extent to which such regulation is consistent with the traditions of the international system;

(g) the extent to which another state may have an interest in regulating the activity;

(h) the likelihood of conflict with regulation by other states.

(3) An exercise of jurisdiction which is not unreasonable according to the criteria indicated in Subsection (2) may nevertheless be unreasonable if it requires a person to take action that would violate a regulation of another state which is not unreasonable under those criteria. Preference between conflicting exercises of jurisdiction is determined by evaluating the respective interests of the regulating states in light of the factors listed in Subsection (2).

(4) Under the law of the United States:

(a) a statute, regulation or rule is to be construed as exercising jurisdiction and applying law only to the extent permissible under § 402 and this section, unless such construction is not fairly possible; but

(b) where Congress has made clear its purpose to exercise jurisdiction which may be beyond the limits permitted by international law, such exercise of jurisdiction, if within the constitutional authority of Congress, is effective as law in the United States.''

338. ''Requests for Disclosure and Foreign Government Compulsion.

(1) (a) Where authorized by statute or rule of court, a court in the United States may order a person before the court to produce documents or other information directly relevant, necessary, and material to an action or investigation, even if the information or the person in possession of the information is located outside the United States.

(b) Failure to comply with an order to produce information may subject the person to whom the order is directed to sanctions, including contempt or dismissal of a claim or defense, or to a finding by the court that the facts to which the order was addressed are as asserted by the opposing party.

(c) In issuing an order directing production of documents or other information located abroad, a court in the United States must take into account the importance to the investigation or litigation of the documents or other information requested; the degree of specificity of the request; in which of the states involved the documents or information originated; the extent to which compliance with the request would undermine important interests of the state where the information is located; and the possibility of alternative means of securing the information.

(2) If disclosure of information located outside the United States is prohibited by a law or regulation of the state in which the information or prospective witness is located, or by the state of nationality of the prospective witness,

(a) the person to whom the order is directed may be required by the court to make a good faith effort to secure permission from the foreign authorities to make the information available;

(b) the court may not ordinarily impose the sanction of contempt, dismissal, or default on the party that has failed to comply with the order for production, except in cases of deliberate concealment or removal of information or of failure to make a good faith effort in accordance with paragraph (a);

(c) the court may, in appropriate cases, make findings of fact adverse to a party that has failed to comply with the order for production, even if that party has made a good faith effort to secure permission from the foreign authorities to make the information available and that effort has been unsuccessful.''

339. Supra note 223 at § 4.05.

340. Declaration of 21 June 1976 on International Investment and Multinational Enterprises, 15 ILM 967 at § 11. The Declaration states at the outset: ''Every State has the right to prescribe the conditions under which multinational enterprises operate within its national jurisdiction, subject to international law and to the international agreements to which it has subscribed. The entities of a multinational enterprise located in various countries are subject to the laws of these countries.''

341. Id. at 972.

342. 480 F Supp 1138 (ND Ill., 1979).

343. 82 A.J.I.L. 521, 555 (1988).

Selected Bibliography to Part I

J. Atwood & K. Brewster, ''Investigations and Discovery,'' in Antitrust and American Business Abroad 214–42 (2d ed. 1981).

Barnard, ''Extra-Territoriality and Anti-Trust Law in the United States,'' 6 Int. & Comp. L.Q. Supp. 95–116 (1963).

Carter, ''Obtaining Foreign Discovery and Evidence for Use in Litigation in the United States: Existing Rules & Procedures,'' 13 Int'l Law, 5–18 (1979).

Deutsch, ''Judicial Assistance: Obtaining Evidence in the United States Under 28 U.S.C. 1782 for Use in a Foreign or International Tribunal,'' 5 B.C. Int'l & Comp. L. Rev. 175–93 (1982).

Griffin, ''Possible Resolutions of International Disputes Over Enforcement of U.S. Antitrust Laws,'' 18 Stan. J. Int'l L. 279–309 (1982).

Grundman, ''New Imperialism: The Extraterritorial Application of United States Law,'' 14 Int'l Law. 257–66 (1980).

Henry, ''U.S. Pretrial Discovery: Extraterritorial Impact on Enforcement and Exploitation of Industrial Property Rights,'' 13 Int'l Rev. Indus. Prop. & Copyright L. 704–28 (1982).

Light, ''Discovery Abroad and the Consequences When Recovery Is Not Possible,'' (National Institute on Critical Issues in International Antitrust and Unfair Competition Law), 50 Antitrust L.J. 577–98 (1982).

Meal & Frachtman, ''Defense to Actions Against Foreign States Under the United States Anti-trust Laws,'' 20 Harv. Int'l L. J. 583–661 (1979).

Note, ''Banking Secrecy and Insider Trading: The U.S.-Swiss Memorandum of Understanding on Insider Trading,'' 23 Va. J. Int'l L. 605–34 (1983).

Note, ''Discovery—Aid to Foreign or International Tribunals—United States

Courts Can Compel Testimony Only on Behalf of Foreign or International Tribunals Empowered to Make Binding Adjudications,'' 7 Vand. J. Transnat'l L. 494–502 (1974).

Note, ''Discovery of Documents Located Abroad in U.S. Antitrust Litigation: Recent Developments in the Law Concerning the Foreign Illegality Excuse for Non-Production,'' 14 Va. J. Int'l L. 747–74 (1974).

O'Kane & O'Kane, ''Taking Depositions Abroad: The Problems Still Remain,'' 31 Fed'n Ins. Counsel Q. 343–59 (1981).

Shemanski, ''Obtaining Evidence in the Federal Republic of Germany: The Impact of the Hague Evidence Convention on German-American Judicial Cooperation,'' 17 Int'l Law. 465–87 (1983).

Stein, ''Depositions in Foreign Jurisdictions—Innocence Abroad,'' 7 Litigation 14–17 (1981).

von Mehren, ''Discovery of Documentary and Other Evidence in a Foreign Country,'' 77 Am. J. Int'l L. 896–902 (1983).

Walsh, ''Service of American Judicial Documents in Foreign Countries,'' 25 Res Gestae 188–90 (1981).

Weintraub, ''Jurisdiction Over the Foreign Non-Sovereign Defendant,'' (Dean Pierre Azard Memorial Symposium), 19 San Diego L. Rev. 431–42 (1982).

PART II

THE NATURE OF THE ABUSES OF THE DISCOVERY PROCESS

11

Abuses of Discovery in General

It is said that abuses of discovery generally may be classified as "overuse" by the plaintiff or the party bringing the suit and "stonewalling" by the defendant or the party defending the suit.[1] The latter may well be the more serious from the viewpoint of the trial itself since stonewalling by the defendant may deprive the plaintiff and the court as well with access to vital and necessary evidence. Stonewalling may take the form of deliberate concealment or nondisclosure of information or documents and can result in such sanctions as the granting of a new trial.[2] Stonewalling is basically an obstructionist tactic: "Objection is made to the interrogatory as being vague, ambiguous, and not reasonably calculated to lead to admissible evidence." Interestingly, in 1985 the U.S. District Court for the Southern District of New York enacted Civil Rule 46 which reads as follows:

(a) At the commencement of discovery, interrogatories will be restricted to those seeking names of witnesses with knowledge or information relevant to the subject matter of the action, the computation of each category of damage alleged, and the existence, custodian, location and general description of relevant documents, including pertinent insurance agreements, and other physical evidence, or information of a similar nature.

(b) During discovery, interrogatories other than those seeking information described in paragraph (a), above may only be served if they are a more practical method of obtaining the information sought than a request for production or a deposition.

(c) At the conclusion of each party's discovery, and prior to the discovery cut-off date, interrogatories seeking the claims and contentions of the opposing party may be served unless the court has ordered otherwise. Questions seeking the names of expert witnesses and the substance of their opinions may also be served, if this information has not been previously obtained.

(d) No part of an interrogatory shall be left unanswered merely because an objection is interposed to another part of the interrogatory.

(e)(1) Where an objection is made to any interrogatory subpart thereof or to any document request under Fed. R. Civ. P. 34, the objection shall state with specificity all grounds. Any ground not stated in an objection within the time provided by Federal Rules of Civil Procedure, or any extensions thereof, shall be waived.

(2) Where a claim of privilege is asserted in objecting to any interrogatory or document demand, or subpart thereof, and an answer is not provided on the basis of such assertion, (i) the attorney asserting the privilege shall in the objection to the interrogatory or document demand, or subpart thereof, identify the nature of the privilege (including work product) which is being claimed and if the privilege is being asserted in connection with a claim or defense governed by state law, indicate the state's privilege rule being invoked; and (ii) the following information shall be provided in the objection, unless divulgence of such information would cause disclosure of the allegedly privileged information:

(A) for documents: (1) the type of document; (2) general subject matter of the document; (3) the date of the document; (4) such other information as is sufficient to identify the document for a subpoena duces tecum, including, where appropriate, the author of the document, the addressee of the document, and, where not apparent, the relationship of the author and adressee to each other;

(B) for oral communications: (1) the name of the person making the communication and the names of persons present while the communication was made and, where not apparent, the relationship of the persons present to the person making the communication; (2) the date and place of communication; (3) the general subject matter of the communication.

(f) Whenever a party answers any interrogatory by reference to records from which the answer may be derived or ascertained, as permitted in Fed. R. Civ. P. 33(c):

(1) The specification of documents to be produced shall be in sufficient detail to permit the interrogating party to locate and identify the records and to ascertain the answer as readily as could the party from whom discovery is sought.

(2) The producing party shall make available any computerized information or summaries thereof that it either has, or can adduce by a relatively simple procedure, unless these materials are privileged or otherwise immune from discovery.

(3) The producing party shall provide any relevant compilations, abstracts or summaries in its custody or readily obtainable by it, unless these materials are privileged or otherwise immune from discovery.

(4) The documents shall be made available for inspection and copying within ten days after service of the answers to interrogatories or at a date agreed upon by the parties.

Civil Rule 46 resulted in virtually eliminating motion practice involving interrogatories in this court! Depositions and document productions were the consequence; overburdening an adversary or sanctioning the delay were somewhat alleviated.[3]

Stonewalling may take the form of incessant delay to increase the plaintiff's litigation costs,[4] hiding of a document with a subsidiary,[5] utilizing a record-keeping indexing system that makes it impossible to locate documents,[6] or downright destruction of documents, presumably to save space.[7] Seeking protective orders purposelessly also increases the time and cost of discovery.[8]

Overuse by zealous plaintiffs is also an abuse of the discovery process, for the sole purpose is to embarrass and "tie-up" the defendant in the discovery process. Overuse by plaintiffs means that the defendants may become more amenable to settlement. Where the defendant sought to subpoena tapes and documents (located all around the country) in the possession of a medical and scientific expert testifying for plaintiffs against the defendant, the New York court in *Matter of R. J. Reynolds Tobacco Co.* repulsed the defendant because "compliance with the subpoena would place an unreasonable burden upon the medical and scientific institutions involved and would unduly disrupt the ongoing research at both Mount Sinai [Hospital] and the American Cancer Society."[9] The defendant was seeking the data in connection with its defense in a California court involving the use of the same tobacco product and the same exposure to asbestos. The subpoenas requested not only tapes and documents but also questionnaires, medical records, death certificates, x-rays, autopsies, computer tapes, and previous or follow-up studies covering the medical investigations (the requested material filled 19 file cabinets and 250 bound volumes, and the data was gleaned from 18,170 people who had been promised confidentiality).[10] The New York court termed the discovery request "sweeping and indiscriminate . . . and oppressive [which would hinder these third parties who] are complete strangers to the underlying litigation."[11]

On the other hand, the federal district court in Wichita, Kansas, in *Graham v. Wyeth Laboratories,* was perfectly willing to compel the defendant product manufacturer to contribute its discovered information and material to a special research library for lawyers and others interested in defendant's vaccine product.[12] The court stated it wanted to make the trial transcript, exhibits, pleadings, depositions, and other pertinent information and documents available because there were more than 200 similar cases pending against the defendant! The court observed that "the record of this case reveals no trade secrets . . . and moreover this company no longer produces the DPT vaccine. It follows that it is in no jeopardy insofar as competitors are concerned."

The New York case of *Hack v. La Chine Classic, Inc.* is a fitting illustration of defendants who failed to comply with the discovery process and who therefore suffered a default judgment.[13] Justice Shainswit of the New York Supreme Court, New York County, at first quoted the trial court's statement to the attorney for the wayward defendants: "This case is an archetype of the abuse of the discovery process. This has been going on for years. . . . Your client has obviously been thumbing his nose at the other side and at the Court. I think that the other counsel has produced ample evidence that invoices were nowhere enough. You have no excuse. I offered you 48 hours to produce the others. You gave me a song and dance off the record about your client being in Korea. There has been one excuse or another for almost two years. . . . The time has come. This is the end. The answer is struck." Justice Shainswit observed that the appellate court here had unanimously affirmed the judgment entered against the defendants in an amount in excess of $136,000. On remand of the case, Justice Shainswit noted that the defendants "obtained a new attorney who claims that his predecessor's advice was wrong, and therefore this court should vacate the judgment, hold a new inquest, and permit defendants to cross-examine plaintiff and offer proof, so as to mitigate damages." But Justice Shainswit refused to consider the request of the new attorney: "The default was not excusable. If prior counsel's advice was wrong, defendants' quarrel is with him; the situation is in no way analogous to law office failure. This was not inadvertence, but a deliberate decision consonant with defendant's entire history of defiance of the court, throughout this case.'' Other defendants have committed abuses of discovery by narrowly interpreting plaintiff's discovery requests, evasive conduct, or by deliberately concealing information or documents.[14]

In *Wynward v. Beiny* the New York Appellate Division, 1st Dept., castigated a New York law firm for abuses of discovery in that it allegedly stole certain documents:[15]

> We do not believe that Sullivan & Cromwell was ignorant of these rules [of discovery] nor would its ignorance be excusable. . . . These are not trivial or seldom invoked provisions; they are fundamental to the orderly and fair conduct of pre-trial litigation and are daily put to use by litigants and the courts. . . . The inference which sadly follows is that, far from making an ''earnest'' attempt to comply with the rules, Sullivan & Cromwell chose to chart a course which it knew to be at variance with acceptable discovery practice so as to obtain by stealth that which could not be readily obtained through proper channels. . . .

This ''blatant abuse,'' which involved ''willful disregard of procedural rules, deceit and the covert acquisition of otherwise unobtainable privileged material,'' prompted removal of the law firm as counsel in this bitter dispute over the rights to at least $20 million of a family's antique porcelain fortune.[16] Another indiscretion by the law firm was termed ''clandestine discovery'' when the law firm failed to give notice of the effort to obtain discovery.[17] Disqualification of the law firm was required,[18] according to the court, ''to protect the integrity of the discovery process,'' and anything less than the law firm's disqualification would invite a reoccurrence of ''a course of activity exhibiting a complete and deliberate disregard for the process by which discovery is to be conducted and a total insensitivity to the strict ethical and legal limitations placed upon the disclosure and use of privileged materials.''[19]

The federal district court in *Thomas E. Hoar, Inc. v. Sara Lee Corp.* was profoundly concerned about the continuing failure of the plaintiff to fulfill its discovery obligations, and upheld the magistrate's order for attorney fees and expenses incurred by defendants: ''Given the history of this case, the court's authority to invoke sanctions is perhaps the most effective means to encourage plaintiff to abandon its persistent disregard of its discovery obligations and to deter further failure to comply with successive orders of the court. . . . [P]laintiff's delaying and obstructionist tactics constitute contemptuous conduct in response to the lawful orders of this court.''[20]

Over 1,000 state and federal judges, responding to a 1988 survey commissioned by Aetna Life and Casualty Co. and conducted by Louis Harris & Associates, have soundly criticized lawyers for abusing discovery and thereby raising litigation costs.[21] At least 90% of the judges who responded said that excessive litigation costs resulted when attorneys ''turn over every stone rather than make cost-benefit analyses of what's useful,'' and that attorneys ''use discovery as an adversarial tool to intimidate opponents.'' National concern with discovery abuses has prompted tightening of discovery rules by the courts,[22] imposing sanctions more aggressively; the U.S. Supreme Court in *National Hockey League v. Metropolitan Hockey Club, Inc.*, encouraged an expanded use of sanctions, not only for remedial purposes but also for deterrence.[23]

12

Spoliation or Destruction of Evidence

In the Arizona case of *LaRaia v. Arizona Superior Court* the issue was whether the injured plaintiff should be granted leave to amend her complaint to allege the tort of "intentional spoliation of evidence."[24] It appears that the defendant had intentionally destroyed the can of pesticide that allegedly caused injuries to the plaintiff. Plaintiff contended that the spoliation or destruction of the relevant evidence hindered her physician's efforts to treat her for injuries resulting from exposure to the organophosphate pesticide, and thereby exacerbated her injuries. Her physician testified that she was improperly treated with atrophine, which was inappropriate for exposure to the particular pesticide then identified (without the availability of the can). The Arizona Supreme Court was unwilling to recognize a new tort of "spoliation of evidence," although the court had found that defendant had acted wrongly:

> [I]f an actor knows or has reason to know that his conduct has caused such bodily injury to another as to make that person helpless and in danger of further harm, the actor is under a duty to exercise reasonable care to prevent such further harm. Because the defendant poisoned the plaintiff, defendant had the duty to minimize the resulting harm after [defendant] discovered what had occurred. Providing correct information as to the nature of the poison was well within the bounds of what could reasonably be expected from the defendant. Spoliation of the evidence only tended to exacerbate the injury, and plaintiff was entitled to amend her complaint to plead such additional injury.

Lost medical records is another example of spoliation or destruction of evidence.[25] It is well-established that courts will not allow a party to benefit from his or her misconduct, and spoliation of evidence is deemed to be an obstruction of justice punishable as a misdemeanor.[26] Lost or missing hospital records can be fatal to a plaintiff's cause of action, as illustrated by *Thor v. Boska.*[27] Here plaintiff had consulted defendant physician about a lump on her breast, but defendant performed no tests and advised her to do nothing about her condition; about eighteen months later, another physician confirmed that she had cancer of the breast. The California appellate court in the medical malpractice suit found that, if the defendant had destroyed his medical record under a consciousness of guilt, such consciousness would be relevant to causation; and, when defendant's negligence makes it impossible for plaintiff to prove proximate causation, it is more appropriate to hold the defendant liable than to deny the innocent plaintiff full recovery. In short, according to the court, defendant's loss of his records should be treated as defeating plaintiff's "burden of proof on causation." Almost a hundred years earlier a Missouri court in *Pomeroy v. Benton* had ruled that "it is because of the very fact that the evidence of the plaintiff, the proofs of his claim or the muniments of his title, have been destroyed by the defendant, that the law, in hatred of the spoiler, baffles the destroyer and thwarts his iniquitous purpose, by indulging a presumption which supplies the lost proof, and thus defeats the wrongdoer by the very means he had so confidently employed to perpetrate the wrong."[28] In *Carr v. St. Paul Fire & Marine Insurance Co.* the federal district court in Arkansas ruled that the jury had the right to infer that missing medical records would favor the plaintiff;[29] it seems here that workers in the hospital's emergency room had destroyed the record of decedent's vital signs. Obviously, plaintiff's decedent was impeded in proving what wrong had been perpetrated by the hospital. In *May v. Moore* the Alabama Supreme Court upheld the admission of evidence that the defendant physician had purposefully destroyed records that supported plaintiff's cause of action, and ruled that the physician's spoliation of the evidence was a sufficient foundation for inferring his guilt or negligence.[30]

In a Florida case the plaintiff seeking sterilization had a tubal ligation performed at the defendant hospital, but about a year and half later she suffered a ruptured ectopic pregnancy.

The operation notes detailing the surgery were not available, and the hospital was granted summary judgment in its favor. On appeal, the Florida Supreme Court ruled that she need only establish that an important hospital record has been lost or destroyed to satisfy her burden of proving that its contents showed the defendant hospital's guilt or negligence.[31] The presumption of spoliation of evidence is not overcome until a jury or court believes that non-negligence has been clearly shown, thus shifting the entire burden of proof to the defendant hospital.[32]

Disappearance of physical evidence is said to have several remedies, to wit: the "adverse inference rule," as described above, implies that the evidence would have been favorable to the other side,[33] and the imposition of sanctions, as illustrated in *William T. Thompson Co. v. General Nutrition Corp.*, where the court imposed a duty to preserve relevant documents, even though not covered by any discovery request.[34]

The spoliation of evidence is an evidentiary presumption that seeks to deter wrongful conduct in the discovery process.[35] One aspect thereof is "redaction" of evidence, i.e., deleting material that is claimed to be irrelevant or privileged. In *U.S. v. Davis* the federal district court for the Southern District of New York ordered that documents be produced to the government without any redactions based on relevancy grounds; the court also ordered that, where documents were redacted on the basis of privilege, the defendants provide the government with a privilege list.[36]

13

Freedom of Information Act and Discovery Abuses

Prior to the 1967 enactment of the Freedom of Information Act, or FOIA,[37] neither the press, the public, nor the litigant had any legal right to demand access to the files of the federal government.[38] FOIA determined to end the practice of federal agencies routinely rejecting citizen requests for information;[39] FOIA established a judicially enforceable public right to know and to secure official information,[40] subject, however, to the well-publicized nine exceptions: (1) classified information; (2) internal personnel rules and practices of federal agencies; (3) exemptions specified in other federal statutes; (4) trade secrets and commercial or financial information obtained from a person and privileged or confidential; (5) interagency or intraagency documents which would not be available in litigation with the agency; (6) personal and medical files and similar files which would constitute a clearly unwarranted invasion of personal privacy; (7) investigatory records compiled for law enforcement purposes under specified conditions; (8) specified data bearing on regulation or supervision of financial institutions; and (9) geological and geophysical information and data, including maps, concerning wells.[41] The U.S. Supreme Court in *Chrysler v. Brown* emphasized FOIA's disclosure mandate which "protects the submitters' interest in confidentiality only to the extent that this interest is endorsed by the agency collecting the information."[42] The first exemption for "classified information" must be substantiated according to Presidential Executive Order No. 12356, issued April 2,

1982, which mandates a uniform system for classifying and safeguarding national security information.[43]

Obviously, the FOIA is a valuable tool in the discovery arsenal, especially in criminal cases, when used in conjunction with discovery obtained under Rules 16 and 17(c) of the Federal Rules of Criminal Procedure for subpoenas and thorough pretrial investigation.[44]

While the FOIA contains provisions to safeguard individual's reputations, the ambit of discovery is such that protection of individual's reputations cannot be guaranteed. The Privacy Act of 1976, which enables individuals to obtain access to certain government records concerning themselves, simply opens the door wider to discovery.[45] The Privacy Act also provides that government agency heads may promulgate regulations to exempt from disclosure any system of records if that system is "maintained by an agency or component thereof which performs as its principal function any activity pertaining to the enforcement of criminal laws, including police efforts to prevent, control, or reduce crime or to apprehend criminals. . . ."[46] States have enacted freedom of information laws too; the New York statute eloquently endorsed the importance of access to information in a free society: "A free society is maintained when government is responsive and responsible to the public, and when the public is aware of governmental actions. The more open a government is with its citizenry, the greater the understanding and participation of the public in government. . . ."[47]

14

Discovery Abuses in the Insurance Field

In the insurance field there are at least two parties actively engaged in discovery, i.e., the insured who claims a right to discover the claims file and other materials from the insurer, and the insurer who requires discovery to present a formidable defense to an action on the insurance policy.[48] From the insured's viewpoint, the insurance company, as illustrated in *United Services Auto Association v. Werley*, cannot invoke a lawyer-client privilege to protect its files if the insured makes a prima facie showing of the insurer's bad-faith failure to pay a claim.[49] Even a third-party plaintiff who has been assigned the insured's cause of action against the insurer may have discovery of the insurer's lawyer's file if that lawyer initially had also represented the insured.[50] The Alabama Supreme Court in *Holt v. State Farm Mutual Automobile Insurance Co.* compelled the insurer to divulge the names and addresses of its insureds who within the past five years filed claims similar to that of the plaintiff insured![51] In *Brown v. Superior Court* the insured sought to compel production of the insurer's claim file in his action for a fire loss to his business.[52] The insurer paid the physical damage loss but refused to pay for business interruption and for loss of accounts receivable and other valuable papers. In his action the insured averred that the insurer and its agents acted in bad faith. The insurer resisted the discovery demand on the ground of irrelevancy, a qualified protection from discovery based on work-product prepared in anticipation of trial, an absolute protection from discovery based on the work-product constituting the mental impressions, conclusions, and legal theories of the insurer's agents and attorneys, and also a privilege relating to the certified public accountant's report.[53] The trial court ordered the insurer to submit the entire claims file for an "in camera" inspection by the court, along with an itemization of the documents and a statement explaining the insurer's position with respect to each document.[54] The insurer reported to the trial court that it was unable to comply because it did not know what documents were requested by the insured. After reviewing the entire claims file the trial court denied plaintiff's motion to compel disclosure; the trial court concluded that much of the data was readily available elsewhere, and much of the data was not discoverable. But the Arizona Supreme Court reversed:

> The tort of bad faith arises when an insurance company intentionally denies, fails to process, or fails to pay a claim without a reasonable basis for such action. . . . No matter how the test is defined, bad faith is a question of reasonableness under the circumstances. . . . The portions of the claims file which explained how the company processed and considered . . . [the insured's] claim and why it rejected the claim are certainly relevant to these issues.
>
> Further, bad-faith actions against an insurer, like actions of client against attorney, patient against doctor, can only be proved by showing exactly how the company processed the claim, how thoroughly it was considered and why the company took the action it did. The claims file is a unique, contemporaneously prepared history of the company's handling of the claim; in an action such as this the need for the information in the file is not only substantial, but overwhelming. . . . The "substantial equivalent" of this material cannot be obtained through other means of discovery. The claims file "diary" is not only likely to lead to evidence, but to be very important evidence on the issue of whether . . . [the insurance company] acted reasonably.

The highest Arizona court concluded by pointing out that

> such protection can [not] be absolute. . . . The reasons the insurance company denied the claim or the manner in which it dealt with it are central issues to the insured's claims of bad faith. Thus, the strategy, theories, mental impressions and opinions of . . . agents concerning the loss of earnings claim are directly at issue. When mental impressions and the like are directly at issue in a case, courts are permitted an exception to the strict protection of Rule 26 (b)(3) and allowed discovery. . . . We emphasize, however, that, this exception will not only be permitted where the material sought to be discovered is

central to a party's claim or defense. Accordingly, we find that the trial court abused its discretion in refusing to permit discovery of the mental impressions, opinion, conclusions, or legal theories of [insurer's] representatives which pertain to the loss of earnings claim and are contained in the claims file.

It is obvious that what is discoverable depends on what is pleaded, and the insured's attorney will frame the complaint against the insurer in those precise terms so as to broaden discovery.[55] Rule 11 of the Federal Rules of Civil Procedure would seemingly be effective in deterring discovery abuses;[56] but it is surprising how infrequently courts invoke the sanction sunder Rule 11.[57] In *Brown v. Nationwide Mutual Insurance Co.*,[58] for example, the sanction of a $1,000 fine under Rule 11 against the attorney was found to be frivolous.[59] Yet Rule 11 does provide punishment if enforced, and when enforced, Rule 11 deters attorneys who plead frivolous claims without reasonable inquiry or sufficient factual basis.[60]

On the other hand, the insurer can maintain a discovery program against the insured; as the federal district court in Delaware pointed out in *McNally v. Nationwide Mutual Insurance Co.*,[61] "Nationwide's need for access to information concerning the plaintiffs' settlement strategy in the litigation is very pressing and . . . Nationwide will be deprived of a fair opportunity to defend this case in the absence of access to this information."[62] And in *Merritt v. Superior Court* the California court held that the injured third-party claimant in a bad-faith failure to settle action was required to respond to the insurer's discovery; neither the attorney-client privilege nor the work-product privilege under the circumstances of the case could bar the insurer's access to discovery of the insured.[63] Here the insurer sought discovery for determination of whether the prior personal injury action was capable of settlement and whether plaintiff's counsel were confused and thereby disabled from settling the case.

In *Allied Bank International v. Fireman's Fund Insurance Co.* the New York court allowed the deposition of plaintiffs' attorneys by the insurance carrier where plaintiffs had brought suit on a fidelity bond for a loss occasioned by the dishonesty of plaintiffs' employees.[64] The insurer was interested in deposing plaintiffs' attorneys with respect to work performed by them prior to the filing of plaintiffs' notice of claim. Plaintiffs' objection to such discovery was based upon the attorney-client privilege; the court ordered the deposition, but only to the extent that it could "contribute relevant, nonprivileged information." The court explained that

> by bringing this action, plaintiff has affirmatively put in issue its entitlement to payment under the bond. Part and parcel of that entitlement is prompt notice; it is a condition precedent to recovery, *Utica Mutual Insurance Co. v. Fireman's Fund Insurance Co.*, 748 F.2d 118 (2nd Cir. 1984). [Applying New York law,] it is immaterial whether timely notice is characterized an affirmative defense or whether it is pleaded by plaintiff, though it is pleaded here. . . . [W]hat counts is not the allocation of issues for pleading and proof purposes, but whether the party asserting the privilege has put the privileged communications "in issue." By making a claim, asserting its timeliness, and suing on it, plaintiff has done so here. . . .

15

Sanctions and Remedies for Discovery Abuse

Sanctions and remedies for discovery abuse run the gamut of the court's discretion and the court's time, and the cases illustrative thereof are legion. In the federal courts, FRCP Rule 11 on signing of pleadings, motions, and other papers[65] and FRCP Rule 37(b) on failure to make or cooperate in discovery[66] delineate the important discovery sanctions. Serious discovery abuses have been penalized severely where there is an absolute refusal to answer interrogatories,[67] incomplete or evasive answers to interrogatories,[68] a pattern of discovery abuses,[69] willful concealment of material facts,[70] fabrication of evidence,[71] or simply a clear refusal to obey court orders on discovery.[72] A survey of recent cases in federal courts would encompass the following.

In *Update Art v. Modiin Publishing Co.* the Second U.S. Court of Appeals backed sanctions against an Israeli news publisher who simply failed to turn over discovery documents.[73] The court issued a "stern warning" in unanimously rejecting an attempt by the defendant to overturn a summary judgment and $476,406 in damages. The court under Rule 37 of FRCP also imposed a $2,000 fine on defendant's attorneys who had "unjustifiably" failed to turn over the requested documents after repeated court orders to do so: "We wish to emphasize the importance we place on a party's compliance with discovery orders. . . . If one suggests that our decision today is strong medicine, that is precisely what it is intended to be."[74]

The intriguing case of *Carlucci v. Piper Aircraft Co.* illustrated how far a court will go before invoking sanctions for discovery abuse.[75] The discovery dispute arose in 1981 following a consolidation of three products liability cases against the defendant; the defendant had apparently violated several discovery orders. Finally, in December 1983 the trial judge found the violations to be shocking because "the defendant had delayed and obstructed discovery to the extent that the case was 5 years old and nowhere near ready for trial."[76] The trial judge wrote 45 pages in his opinion detailing the bad faith and obstructionist tactics of the defendant. A subsequent evidentiary hearing revealed that defendant had either disposed of vital documents or had intentionally withheld them from plaintiff and the court; defendant had objected to discovery by its attorney as burdensome but the attorney never consulted the client to attest to that singular conclusion.[77] Defendant had even objected to producing certain documents, then had later denied the documents existed.[78] A memorandum of law from defendant had misrepresented that plaintiff had acknowledged production of numerous documents from defendant.[79] Thereupon, the court entered a default judgment against the defendant: "Deliberate, willful and contumacious disregard of the judicial process and the rights of opposing parties justifies the most severe sanction. The policy of resolving lawsuits on their merits must yield when a party has intentionally prevented the fair adjudication of the case. By deliberately destroying documents, the defendant has eliminated the plaintiff's right to have their cases decided on the merits. Accordingly, the entry of a default is the only means of effectively sanctioning the defendant and remedying the wrong." Finally, the court struck defendant's pleading, entered a finding of liability, and ordered the case to trial solely on the issue of the amount of damages to be awarded to the plaintiff. It should be noted that Rule 37(b)(2)(C) of FRCP authorizes dismissal of actions for failure to obey an order to permit discovery. On appeal, the Eleventh U.S. Court of Appeals affirmed the sanctions, but remanded the case to determine how the trial court had arrived at a $10,000 sanction against one of the defendant's lawyers for obstruction of discovery and violation of court orders.[80]

In *McCarthy v. Philippine National Bank* the federal district court for the Southern District of New York granted defendant's motion to strike plaintiff's quantum meruit claim for legal fees in the amount of $1.8 million;[81] plaintiff had rendered legal services to the defendant in a dispute between the defendant and the Internal Revenue Service.

The court's sanction was based upon a finding that plaintiff had repeatedly violated orders of production by failing to produce contemporaneous time records he had maintained in which he noted the items worked on and the amount of time he devoted to the item; also, while plaintiff was delaying production of the diary entries it was found that he was also altering the diary entries. The court concluded that plaintiff "willfully ignored his discovery obligations and specifically disobeyed the Magistrate's discovery orders." In *Corona v. A-B-C Packaging Machine Corp.* the New York Appellate Division, 2nd Dept., struck the answer of the third-party defendant Coca-Cola because "Coca-Cola was aware of a prior order of the same court compelling the inspection of the machine, but nevertheless had it destroyed."[82] The sanction imposed, "although a severe one, cannot be said to be an abuse of the court's broad discretion."[83]

In *Hull v. Waterbury Petroleum Products* the Second U.S. Court of Appeals ruled that the federal district court may under Rule 37 direct that a complaint be dismissed where a party flagrantly disregarded court discovery orders.[84] Here defendant apparently failed to comply with three orders "requiring it to completely and fully answer [third-party defendant's] interrogatories and to specify the basis for its counterclaim damages." In affirming the dismissal of the complaint, the court pointed out:

> The imposition of sanctions under Rule 37 is within the discretion of the district court and a decision to dismiss an action for failure to comply with discovery orders will only be reversed if the decision constitutes an abuse of that discretion . . . the record demonstrated that [the district court] was fully justified in dismissing Waterbury's complaint for its failure to provide discovery to [the third-party defendant]. . . .[Waterbury failed] to provide any meaningful discovery concerning a core trial issue, despite three clear court orders, which included two warnings that dismissal would follow if Waterbury failed to provide adequate responses to the request.

The court also ordered Waterbury to pay $27,500 in fees and expenses incurred by the third-party defendant in pursuing this action.[85]

Sanctions for federal discovery abuses or violations are also found in Rule 16(d)(2) of the Federal Rules of Criminal Procedure. For the government's failure to provide discovery, the trial court may order immediate production of the undisclosed evidence, grant a continuance, prohibit the introduction into evidence of the undisclosed material, or enter any other order it deems just.[86] However, in *United States v. Jackson,*[87] the Seventh U.S. Court of Appeals upheld the dismissal of the indictment because the government failed to provide the defendant with a list of witnesses pursuant to the order of the trial court.[88]

It should be observed that FRCP 11 is indifferent to the subjective mental state of an alleged offender,[89] and relates to misconduct such as the signing of a pleading, motion, or other paper in discovery that is not well-grounded in fact and in law.[90] The 1983 amendment of Rule 11 eliminated the requirement that bad faith had to be shown before sanctions could be imposed, and thereupon enhanced the judicial use of the sanctions.[91] The sanctions are mandatory where there is a clear violation of Rule 11,[92] whether the offender be a lawyer, client, or both.[93] Note that Rule 11 applies only to papers actually served or filed during federal court proceedings; it would not apply, for example, to settlement agreements that are not filed with the court for approval.[94]

FRCP Rule 37 is activated generally by a party's refusal to comply with a court order. Contempt proceedings may result; and, if so, contempt may take the form of a fine for criminal contempt, a compensatory award in favor of the party harmed by the discovery abuse for civil contempt, or coercive contempt, which is a civil remedy designed to secure the conduct from the contemnor that the court had originally ordered.[95] Of course, preclusion orders, as delineated above, are always available to the court, especially where there is clear evidence of discovery abuse. Preclusion orders take into consideration (a) whether the other party has been prejudiced, (b) whether the prejudice can be cured, (c) how important the evidence is or was, (d) the good or bad faith of the violator, and (e) the potential for abuse if the evidence or the issue is not precluded.[96]

In addition to FRCP Rules 11 and 37 as described above, discovery abuses may be curbed by other pretrial sanctions and remedies. For example, Rule 26(g) applies the strictures of Rule 11 to all discovery requests, responses, and objections. FRCP Rule 30(g)(2) also supplies a remedy for a specific form of discovery abuse in the form of an award of attorney fees to reimburse a party attending a deposition if a witness who was subpoenaed failed to appear. FRCP Rule 16(f), at least since the 1983 amendments, mandates that attorney fees be awarded if a party or counsel fails to obey a scheduling order or a pretrial order, or fails to attend a scheduling or pretrial conference, or attends the conference but is "substantially unprepared" to participate in the conference, or simply fails to participate in good faith.[97] Still other FRCP rules that are pertinent include Rule 56(g) on contempt, costs, and attorney fees as a sanction for filing affidavits in bad faith, and Rule 41(b-d) on involuntary dismissal and assessment of costs for failure to prosecute or to comply with the rules or order of the court. Another interesting statute is 28 USC 1972, which is aimed directly at lawyers who ignore its provisions by "multiplying" the discovery proceedings "unreasonably and vexatiously"; the violator "may be required by the court to satisfy personally the excess costs, expenses, and attorneys' fees reasonably incurred because of such conduct." The provisions of 28 USC 1972 apply to all cases and all proceedings out of the federal courts.[98]

Monetary sanctions against an attorney under FRCP Rule 11 are immediately appealable as a collateral order, but the imposition of the sanction must be preceded by notice and an opportunity to be heard, accompanied by an explanation of the reasons, according to the Second U.S. Court of Appeals in *Sanko Steamship Co., Ltd. v. Galin.*[99]

At the state level the following cases spell out the requisites for sanctions:

1. In *Far Out Music, Inc. v. Jordan* the Florida court entered default judgment against the defendant, who did not comply with discovery orders; the court ruled that the default judgment could be entered, following notice and hearing.[100] The defendant's adamant refusal to obey the discovery orders prevented the plaintiffs from establishing a case for compensatory damages, thereby justifying an award of punitive damages also.

2. In *Paris v. Waterman Steamship Corp.* the New York Appellate Division, 1st Dept., imposed "a stiff monetary sanction upon defendant's counsel," but refused to sanction the striking of defendant's answer.[101] According to the court

> In the middle of a trial that had already been brought to the verge of mistrial on numerous occasions by the deplorable antics of counsel for both sides, plaintiff's counsel leaped to his feet and in the presence of the jury began to accuse defendant's counsel of trickery and deceit. So exercised did plaintiff's counsel become that he began to rip parts of an exhibit. A mistrial was of necessity declared.

Thereafter, it came to light that defendant's counsel, at the time of plaintiff's counsel's outburst, had been attempting to cross-examine the plaintiff, using copies of annual medical examinations performed by plaintiff's Union, the Seafarer's International Union (SIU). Despite a stipulation executed by the parties to conduct open disclosure, and the pertinent rules of the CPLR directed toward the same end, defendant's counsel it appeared had, unbeknownst to plaintiff or his counsel, obtained copies of the aforementioned plaintiff's medical records and had then sought to introduce them surreptitiously into the proceeding. Although defendant's counsel initially maintained steadfastly that the records had been received from the plaintiff's camp, subsequent investigation revealed that some years before someone in defendant's counsel's office had subpeonaed the records from the SIU and, indeed, that no one else had sought the records until the time of the judicial subpoena issued by the court in the course of performing its own inquiry of the matter. The court, appropriately appalled by these very serious disclosures respecting the covert manner in which the medical records had been obtained and secreted from plaintiff's counsel despite the parties' stipulation, ruled upon an outstanding motion by plaintiff and determined that defendant's answer should be struck and the matter set down for an inquest as to damages. In so ruling, the court made no express finding that the conduct of defendant's counsel was deliberate. Rather, the factor emphasized by the court in directing that the answer be struck was that the action had already been pending over a decade and that plaintiff had been prejudiced by the delay.

While we take a very serious view of defendant's counsel's apparent failure to honor the rules governing the conduct of *discovery* and the solemn stipulation entered into by the parties, we do not think that the *sanction* of striking defendant's answer was appropriate under the circumstances. As noted, the court made no actual finding that defendant's attorney had deliberately engaged in falsification, or that the medical records had been obtained with his knowledge. Without such a finding, the sanction of striking a defendant's answer is not warranted.

The court concluded that "moreover, we cannot help but observe in assessing the propriety of the sanction imposed, that plaintiff's attorney behaved most inappropriately throughout the proceeding and himself failed to disclose as he should have the identity of an expert medical witness he called to testify.

Last, we do not think that the delay in resolving this case is entirely the fault of defendant's counsel. It should be remembered that, provoked or not, the behavior of plaintiff's counsel in bringing about a mistrial was inexcusable."

3. *Stavola v. Esmail Falaz* involved defendant's motion to dismiss a medical malpractice action on the ground that plaintiff intentionally answered interrogatories falsely.[102] The Connecticut Practice Book Section 231, setting forth the sanctions which can be imposed, delineates "permissible sanctions" as ranging from entry of a nonsuit to entry of a judgment of dismissal. Among the factors to be considered are whether the party's violation was inadvertent or willful, the importance of the information requested to the other party's case, and which sanction would be an appropriate response to the disobedient party's conduct. The core of plaintiff's difficulty here was the identification as her expert witness of a physician who had not agreed to testify! The court concluded that the most satisfactory and appropriate response to plaintiff's conduct was to enter a judgment dismissing the case. This sanction will also deter other litigants from playing fast and loose with the discovery process in Connecticut, according to the court.

The thrust or objective of discovery sanctions in the ordinary case is to obtain information, not to effect a punishment, so that frequently a moving party will not request any sanction in exchange for the vital information. A moving party may seek a substantial monetary fine, not with any realization of the fine being expected, but to impress on the court the unreasonableness of the opponent's refusal to provide the requested discovery materials.

16

The Intentional Tort of Discovery Abuse or Spoliation

It is said that discovery is the one category of litigation conduct where intentional violations are almost accepted as unwritten rules of the game.[103] While Rule 11 of the Federal Rules of Civil Procedure would appear to deter discovery abuses,[104] it should be observed that discovery requests and responses are also evaluated under Rule 26(g), which is designed to curb harassing or redundant discovery and discovery disproportionate to the stakes of a dispute. Rule 37 primarily regulates failures to participate in discovery by the contempt order or by fines amounting to the other party's expenses and attorneys' fees or even dismissal of the case in the first place. Rule 16(f) grants the trial judge vast authority to sanction failures in the pretrial process generally.[105] But these statutory enactments as interpreted and enforced by the federal judiciary have simply not served as meaningful deterrents to curb discovery abuse. It is therefore proposed that an intentional tort of discovery abuse or spoliation be recognized.[106]

There is a Latin maxim, "omnia praesumtur contra spoliatorem," or all will be presumed against the destroyer of evidence, which is spelled out in these terms: "if a plaintiff by his own act fails to furnish a court with important evidence concerning his claim, the court will not hesitate to draw inference against him."[107] In the Australian case of *Saloustic v. Nikic,*[108] the court observed that the plaintiff, after signing the contract and paying a deposit "destroyed the only copy of the agreement, intending to terminate the contract and dispose of the documentary evidence concerning its provisions.''[109] The Australian court thereupon stated: ''The general principle is that where a person intentionally puts it out of his power to produce something which he could produce, the object or article being of a nature relevant to the claim or defence, the principle . . . will cause an unfavourable inference to be drawn against that person.''[110] Indeed, where there is an intentional act of evidence suppression or spoliation of evidence, the tort of discovery abuse should be universally recognized. In the landmark 1984 decision by the California Court of Appeals, *Smith v. Superior Court*, the tort of discovery abuse was fully recognized.[111]

Here plaintiff Smith was driving her automobile when another vehicle's left rear wheel and tire flew off and crashed through the windshield of the Smith automobile; the impact caused pieces of glass to strike her in the eyes and face causing permanent blindness in both eyes and an impairment of her sense of smell. The automobile dealer for the other car, while initially agreeing with plaintiff to maintain certain automobile parts as physical evidence,[112] ''destroyed, lost or transferred said physical evidence, making it impossible for the Smith's experts to inspect and test those parts in order to pinpoint the cause of the failure of the wheel assembly'' on the other car.[113] Plaintiff thereupon petitioned successfully for a writ of mandate seeking relief from the sustaining of a demurrer to the cause of action. The court held that it was appropriate to recognize a new tort for the intentional spoliation of evidence where the underlying litigation had not yet come to trial,[114] so that no collateral estoppel issue existed.[115] The court pointed out that the harm suffered by the plaintiff was different from the harm suffered by the public by the destruction of evidence; the statute making it a misdemeanor to destroy or conceal documentary evidence did not provide a sufficient deterrent,[116] and plaintiff's case was significantly prejudiced by the destruction of the evidence, even though the underlying personal injury litigation had not yet gone to trial and the damages could not be stated with certainty.[117] The California appellate court recognized the tort of discovery abuse as ''closely analogous'' to ''intentional interference with prospective business advantage.''[118] The court concluded: ''While intentional spoliation of evidence has not yet been recognized as a tort heretofore . . . a prospective civil action is a valuable 'probable expectancy' that the court must protect from the kind of interference alleged herein.''

Spoliation is definable as the destruction or alteration of evidence without the consent of all interested parties.[119] The new tort of discovery abuse is based upon an intentional act, although the earlier California decision in *Williams v. State of California* suggested that the tort could be based upon negligence.[120] The Williams case, strange as it may seem, like *Smith v. Superior Court,* involved an automobile and an injury to the plaintiff when a piece of heated brake drum from a passing truck flew into her windshield and struck her in the face before coming to rest on the rear seat of her automobile.[121] Plaintiff alleged that the police officers who arrived on the scene negligently failed to secure the identification of witnesses, negligently failed to test the brake drum part to determine whether it was still hot, and negligently failed to attempt investigation or pursuit of the owner or operator of the truck. The California Supreme Court, in reversing the trial court's dismissal against the State of California based on sovereign immunity, directed the trial court to permit plaintiff to file an amended complaint with a cause of action for negligent spoliation or destruction of evidence. The court observed that, while there is no special relationship between police officers and an injured plaintiff on the public highway which calls for a duty to act carefully, there may be a protective duty assumed toward a certain member of the public if action is undertaken which induces reliance thereupon by the member of the public.[122]

The intentional tort of discovery abuse or spoliation[123] has apparently received approval on the appellate level in Alaska, Arizona, California, Florida, Georgia, Illinois, Kansas, and Maryland.[124] In the Florida case of *Bondu v. Gurvich* recognition was given to an action for *negligent* destruction of evidence.[125] Here plaintiff had brought a medical malpractice action against the hospital for the death of her husband. The hospital, when requested to produce the medical records, stated that the medical records could not be found. Plaintiff's complaint asserted that the hospital had purposefully and intentionally lost and/or destroyed the medical records, thereby precluding her from offering that evidence to prove her case. The trial court nevertheless entered summary judgment in favor of the hospital due to lack of medical records. A subsequent suit (with damages certain) prompted the Florida court to find that "an action should lie against a defendant which, as here, stands to benefit by the fact that the prospect of successful litigation against it has disappeared along with the crucial evidence."[126] Tort liability, whether based on intentional acts or merely negligence, creates a strong deterrent against spoliation or destruction of evidence beyond statutory penalties. An individual or company would no longer be able to escape liability by destroying evidence before a legal proceeding was instituted or by claiming lack of knowledge that a legal proceeding might be subsequently instituted.[127] Recognition of the tort of discovery abuse would alleviate any ethical confusion lawyers might have about advising clients to destroy or "stonewall" evidence.

The Alaska Supreme Court in *Hazen v. Municipality of Anchorage* found a common law action in tort for intentional interference with a prospective civil action by spoliation of evidence:[128] "In recognizing this 'new tort' we find persuasive the reasoning in Smith v. Superior Court. . . . Hazen's prospective false arrest and malicious prosecution actions were valuable, probable expectancies. If the arrest tape was intentionally altered, this was an unreasonable interference with those expectancies that can be remedied in tort."[129] The existence of a criminal penalty for the wrong should not "interfere" with the civil tort for the same conduct.[130] Also it would appear that the new tort should relax the traditional standards of intent, causation, and damages, requiring:[131] (a) proof only that the defendant intentionally spoliated evidence, not that defendant intentionally interfered with plaintiff's suit; (b) proof only that a reasonable probability existed as to proximate cause, not that plaintiff would have obtained compensation "but for" the interference; and (c) proof only that damages resulted, not that the amount of damages are reasonably certain.[132]

Admittedly, recognition of the tort of intentional spoliation of evidence or discovery abuse may increase litigation since both sides to litigation might sue for the new tort. But most courts will respect the test of "significant prejudice" as a basis for the new tort, i.e., the new tort should be permitted only in those cases in which the property destroyed constitutes potential evidence without which proof of an essential element of the cause of action is rendered unreasonably difficult. In a products liability suit the destruction or loss of the product leaves the injured plaintiff with no direct evidence to prove the product's defect. But in a medical malpractice case the destruction of the medical records may not prove fatal if there is other evidence as to the attending physician's or the hospital's negligence.[133] Inadvertent destruction of a paper bag containing bottle fragments in a lawyer's office by the building janitor was not "spoliation" because the destruction of such evidence in the products liability case was unforeseeable.[134] However, there remains the legal aphorism that evidence destroyed or lost by the litigant is presumed to have been adverse to the spoliator.[135]

The 1986 District of Columbia case of *Hinkle v. Sam Blanken & Co.* adopted the view that delay resulting from violations of discovery rules can be so prejudicial as to warrant dismissal of the case.[136] The court observed that the discovery violation was "willful" and "prejudiced" the party seeking discovery.[137] Citing the U.S. Supreme Court decision in *National Hockey League v. Metropolitan Hockey Club,*[138] where there were repeated, flagrant failures to answer interrogatories,[139] the District of Columbia court substantiated its dismissal of the case as a method of deterrence of discovery abuse.[140] Here the dire penalty of dismissal of the case might not have resulted if the District of Columbia had recognized the intentional tort of discovery abuse and granted relief based upon damages therefrom in the separate cause of action.[141]

The recognition of a prospective personal injury action as a legally protected "probable expectancy" is consistent with general tort principles. As Professor Prosser has observed, the law of torts "is directed toward the compensation of individuals . . . for the losses which they have suffered in respect of all their legally recognized interests."[142] The benefits of recognizing a tort cause of action for the intentional spoliation of evidence outweigh any burdens that may result to potential defendants.[143] The new tort promotes the public interest by enhancing the administration of justice and by deterring the destruction of evidence; it promotes the private interest by providing an injured plaintiff with a realistic opportunity to receive compensation for injuries. Thus, spoliation of evidence is an act that constitutes both a crime against the state and a tort against the individual.[144] It is not fruitful to look only at the criminal deterrent when there is an effective tort deterrent in the form of the cause of action for the intentional tort of discovery abuse. The analogy to the tort for intentional interference with a prospective economic advantage rings true, for in the intentional tort of discovery abuse there exists the potential economic relationship, defendant's knowledge of the relationship, interference therewith, intentional conduct, causation between the interference and the injury, and the resulting damages.[145] The obvious limitation on the cause of action for intentional spoliation of evidence is that the evidence itself must be relevant or material to the winning or losing of the underlying lawsuit.[146]

The U.S. Supreme Court on January 25, 1988 in *Taylor v. Illinois,* an attempted murder case, approved the trial court prohibiting defense witnesses from testifying at a criminal trial in order to punish the defendants' lawyers for their discovery violations.[147] The discovery abuse in the Illinois criminal trial involved a defense witness whom the defense attorney "lied about" to the court: the witness was actually visited by the defense attorney the week before the trial began, but the defense attorney informed the court that he wanted to produce at trial now that witness whom he had been unable to locate! The Illinois trial court labeled the "lie" a "blatant" discovery rule violation, and as sanction excluded the defense witness' testimony. The highest court held that the sanction was not absolutely prohibited by the compulsory process clause of the Sixth Amendment: "The accused does not have an unfettered right to offer testimony that is incompetent, privileged or otherwise inadmissible under standard rules of evidence. The compulsory process clause provides him with an effective weapon, but it is a weapon that cannot be used irresponsibly. . . . Whenever a lawyer makes use of the sword provided by the compulsory process clause, there is some risk that he may wound his own client."[148]

The intentional tort of discovery abuse or spoliation may require legislation to augment the decisional base for the tort.

Notes to Part II

1. See Hare, ReMine, and Gilbert, ''Abuses in Discovery'', National Law Journal (July 20, 1987) at 28 et seq.

2. See, for example, Rozier v. Ford Motor Co., 573 F2d 1332 (5th Cir. 1978).

3. See National Law Journal (July 11, 1988) at 1 et seq. Also see O'Brien v. Lane Bryant, Inc., unreported (SDNY, 1987).

4. See Shelton v. American Motors, 106 FRD 490 (W. Ark., 1985) rev'd 805 F2d 1323 (8th Cir., 1986).

5. Note Carey Canada, Inc. v. Hinely, 352 SE2d 398 (Ga App. 1986).

6. See generally In re Agent Orange Product Liability Litigation, 506 F Supp 750 (EDNY, 1980).

7. See generally 61 Texas L Rev 1185 (1983).

8. See Williams v. Johnson & Johnson, 50 FRD 31 (SDNY, 1970).

9. 518 NYS2d 729 (New York County, August 6, 1987).

10. According to the court, ''A subpoena should readily identify the material sought with reasonable precision depending upon the individual case. Enumeration of documents may, however, not be necessary and a class description may be sufficient. (Hale v. Henkel, 201 U.S. 43; Matter of Sun-Ray Cloak Co., Inc., 256 AD 620; Smith v. Russo-Asiatic Bank, 170 Misc. 408; Matter of Trombetta v. Van Amringe, 156 Misc. 307, 310). Reynold's subpoenae, however, are not selective. Rather, they are sweeping and indiscriminate.

A subpoena may be challenged on the grounds that it is overbroad, burdensome or oppressive (Matter of La Belle Creole International, S.A. v. Attorney General, 19 NY2d 192; Wehringer v. Volvo of America Corporation, 55 AD2d

558, (1976); Cunningham and Kaming, P.C. v. Nadjari, 53 AD2d 520). A subpoena may be vacated for reasons of privileges, whether statutory or constitutional, or having its genesis under common law (see People v. Iannacone, 112 Misc. 2d 1057, dealing with Civil Rights Law §79-h [commonly referred to as the Shield Law]; McGowan v. Metropolitan Life Insurance Company, 234 AD 366, app. dismissed 259 N.Y.454, dealing with the Department of Health and records of communicable diseases).

CPLR 3101 provides that '[t]here shall be a full disclosure of all evidence . . . ,' which means all relevant information calculated to lead to relevant evidence (West v. Aetna Casualty and Surety Co. 49 Misc. 2d 28, 29). The data requested must be material and necessary although it need not be indispensable (Aline v. Crowell–Collier Publishing Co. 21 NY2d 403, 407). The rules of evidence may be considered when determining necessity of the requested material. But inadmissibility by itself may not be reason for denying access to the information, since such information may lead to evidence. In addition, its use in cross-examination can be a consideration. . . .

However, when compliance with subpoenae would be so oppressive as to hinder the normal functioning of a Department of the medical school and/or of the American Cancer Society for a prolonged period of time, the Court on motion or on its own initiative may provide appropriate relief.

This is especially so because Mt. Sinai and the American Cancer Society are complete strangers to the underlying litigation. Neither Dr. Selikoff nor his co-authors will be witnesses at the Page trial. They are not consultants in that matter, nor was decedent Page a subject of their medical investigation. . . .

Policy in New York, unlike most other jurisdictions, has accorded privilege to experts (see, People ex. rel. Kraushaar Bros. v. Thorpe, 296 N.Y. 223, holding that an expert cannot be compelled to give his opinion as an expert against his will). The United States Supreme Court held in the notable case of Branzburg v. Hayes, (3408 U.S. 665, 688 [1972]) 'that "the public has a right to every man's evidence," except for those persons protected by a constitutional, common law or statutory privilege.' (citing United States v. Bryan 339 U.S. 323 at 331).

If the production of the material would become oppressive and unreasonably burdensome, the court, in balancing the hardships, should consider whether there are other sources for obtaining the material needed to disprove the conclusions reached by the three studies. In addition, the probative value of the material, if produced, should be considered."

11. The court concluded: "In balancing competing values in this medical area the question presented is whether the tobacco industry, after years of inactivity, should be permitted to salvage their legal defenses at the expense of some of the world's leading medical investigators. . . .

Reynolds has offered to reimburse Mt. Sinai and the American Cancer Society for the reasonable expenses incurred in their complying with the subpoenae. However, it appears that Dr. Selikoff and his colleagues would still have to spend over a thousand hours of time removing the data identifying the individuals who participated in the study. The loss of the scientists' time in complying with the subpoenae would be an unreasonable burden and would unduly interrupt their ongoing medical investigations.

It is also clear that the medical material requested is not of an archival nature but rather is in constant use as part of ongoing medical research.

Reynold's actual need for the material appears to be seriously diminished by the statement in its Reply papers that 'Mount Sinai and the American Cancer Society are well aware that the mass of material accumulated by Dr. Selikoff and his colleagues during the course of the studies is *not needed by Reynolds to evaluate the studies' conclusions*' (emphasis supplied). . . .

Mount Sinai and the American Cancer Society protest, on behalf of their medical scientists, the interference with their ongoing scientific research in this area. While these medical investigations are still in progress, they should not be subjected to examination and criticism by people whose interests are arguably antithetical to the medical scientists. It would have the effect of denying to these doctors the opportunity of first publication of their studies. It could also have a chilling effect and discourage future scientific endeavors.

Mount Sinai, the American Cancer Society, the Dean at the Yale University School of Medicine, and other eminent medical scholars claim that forced compliance with the subpoenae would result in an interference with their academic freedom. It was stated in Dow Chemical Co. v. Allen, 672 F.2d 1262, 1275 (1982) that 'whatever constitutional protection is afforded by the First Amendment extends as readily to the scholar in the laboratory as to the teacher in the classroom.' Of course, like all other constitutional rights, academic freedom is not absolute and must be balanced against competing interests (see, e.g. Barenblatt v. United States, 360 U.S. 109). For present purposes, respondent's interest in academic freedom may properly figure into the legal calculation of whether forced disclosure would be reasonable.

For the reasons stated above, the court finds that compliance with the subpoenae would place an unreasonable burden upon the medical and scientific institutions involved and would unduly disrupt the ongoing research at both Mount Sinai and the American Cancer Society."

12. 666 F Supp 1483 (Kan., November 2, 1987). See also National Law Journal (February 22, 1988) at 1.

13. Unreported (New York County, January 6, 1988).

14. Note, for example, Gammon v. Clark Equipment Co., 686 P2d 1102 (Wash. App., 1985), aff 707 P2d 685 (Wash., 1985).

15. Unreported (1st Dept., June 18, 1987). Note the report in the New York Times (June 28, 1987) at 27.

16. See New York Law Journal (June 23, 1987) at 1 et seq.

17. ''Although Sullivan & Cromwell professes to know of no rule preventing it from using an attorney's subpoena, as it did, to compel the clandestine production of documents from a non-party who is not to be deposed, the law is otherwise. CPLR 3120(b) sets forth the proper procedure for obtaining discovery and production without deposition from a non-party: *'R 3120 Discovery and production of documents and things for inspection, testing, copying or photographing. . . .* (b) As against non-party. A person not a party may be directed by order to do whatever a party may be directed to do under subdivision (a). *The motion for such order shall be on notice to all adverse parties; the non party shall be served with the notice of motion in the same manner as a summons.'* (emphasis added).

We do not think that this provision, designed to assure that non-parties will not be unduly burdened with discovery demands and that discovery from non-parties is conducted in a fair and open manner, can be avoided by resorting to the use of covertly issued attorney's subpoenas. . . . Sullivan & Cromwell's contention to the contrary is not worthy of further comment.

The above-cited rules governing the conduct of discovery and dictating that parties be notified of deposition and disclosure demands made upon non-parties, are well known. Indeed, as the Surrogate observed in her decision disposing of the Trustee's original motion, '[i]t is hornbook law that a party is entitled to a notice of deposition when a subpoena is served on a non-party witness.' We do not believe that Sullivan & Cromwell was ignorant of these rules, nor would its ignorance be excusable. These are not trivial or seldom invoked provisions; they are fundamental to the orderly and fair conduct of pretrial litigation and are daily put to use by litigants and the courts.

Faced with these substantive and procedural impediments to the rapid and sweeping disclosure it was after, Sullivan & Cromwell apparently resolved to avoid the frustration of the adversary process and treat discovery as a private matter between it and the Greenbaum liquidator. It is, of course, undisputed that in March, 1985, Beeney initiated private telephone contacts with Wiener during which Beeney proposed that Sullivan & Cromwell be permitted access to files covering those matters in which the Greenbaum firm had represented the Weinbergs. We note that Beeney made this request knowing full well that the files he asked to examine had been generated over the course of more than ten years of legal representation, and that they certainly contained much in the way of privileged material. When Wiener refused Beeney's request which was nothing more than an invitation to divulge client confidences in violation of CPLR 4503(a) and Disciplinary Rule 4-101, noting at the time of his refusal that he had no authorization from anyone, and in particular from the executor of the Weinberg estate, to release the files, Beeney attempted to elicit Wiener's cooperation by slightly different, but no less private means.

The covertly served March 8, 1985 subpoena duces tecum followed, accompanied by the cover letter representing that petitioner Wynyard on whose behalf the subpoena was issued 'is the executor and an heir to Mr. Weinberg's will. . . .' The natural effect of this representation was to create the impression that Wynyard as executor of the Weinberg estate had authorized the release of the Greenbaum files. Of course, as Beeney well knew, the Weinberg will had never been probated and Wynyard, therefore, had never been appointed executor of the Weinberg estate. While it is questionable whether even a duly appointed executor would have had the power to waive the decedent's attorney-client privilege (see, *Matter of Williams,* 179 Misc 805; *Matter of Alexander,* 205 Misc 894; but see *Matter of Fishman,* 32 AD 2d 1063 aff'd 27 NY 2d 8089), it is quite certain that one merely named as executor in an unprobated will would have had no authority whatsoever to do so. Wynyard's status then as a named executor in an unprobated will was utterly irrelevant to the legitimacy of the disclosure demand made in the subpoena duces tecum. It is, therefore, exceedingly difficult to understand why petitioner's counsel found it worthy of mention in the March 8, 1985 cover letter, if not to mislead Wiener whose cooperation was essential to the conduct of secret discovery, into believing that the authorization for the release of the Greenbaum files, which he previously indicated was lacking, had in fact been given. Certainly, the highly deceptive nature of the representation is self-evident.

When Wiener, whose account of what transpired we find completely creditworthy, was still reluctant to make the files available without Mrs. Beiny's authorization, Beeney again resorted to deception to elicit Wiener's quiet cooperation; Wiener was assured by Beeney that the files would be made available to Mrs. Beiny's attorneys. Thus assured, Wiener retrieved the files and had them delivered to Sullivan & Cromwell. As subsequent events demonstrate beyond doubt, Beeney had not the slightest intention of making the files available to the Trustee or her counsel.

The object of Sullivan & Cromwell's clandestine discovery having been attained without any of the unpleasantness or frustration which would have resulted had the applicable provisions of the CPLR been complied with, Wiener's deposition was promptly cancelled. Thereafter, the files were retained by Sullivan & Cromwell. No effort was made to notify the Trustee that the files were in Sullivan & Cromwell's possession. Indeed, that obviously would have been contrary to Sullivan & Cromwell's purpose. . . ."

18. "It is important to stress that the rationale for the disqualification here imposed is not fundamentally different from that employed in situations where an attorney undertakes to represent interests adverse to those of a former or present client. What is to be prevented is the misuse of information disclosed in confidence between attorney and client. (See *Board of Education v. Nyquist,* 590 F.2d 1241, 1246 [2d Cir. 1981].) While the question of disqualification ordinarily arises when the same attorney or firm represents or has represented parties whose interests are adverse in related matters, as the present case demonstrates, this is not the only factual configuration in which infor-

mation divulged to an attorney in confidence may come to be used for unauthorized ends. (See *e.g. Fund of Funds, Ltd. v. Arthur Andersen & Co.*, 567 F.2d 225 [2d Cir. 1977]; *Cinema 5, Ltd. v. Cinerama, Inc.*, 528 F.2d 1384 [2d Cir. 1977]; *Desbiens v. Ford Motor Co.*, supra.) Here Sullivan & Cromwell has clandestinely obtained the entire files of the Greenbaum firm generated over more than ten years respecting matters in which it represented the Weinberg interests and has used the information thus acquired, much of which is confidential, to advance litigational ends unsanctioned by Greenbaum's clients. Clearly, this sort of abuse of confidential information, whether by the original attorney or one of whom the information has been illicitly transferred, cannot be countenanced. It is serious enough when client privilege is compromised, but when the information obtained as a consequence is then put to use in legal proceedings to prejudice one of those whose confidences have been revealed (here the Trustee) the sanction of disqualification must be imposed. This is necessary not only to sanitize the proceeding but to prevent the offending lawyer or firm from deriving any further benefit from information obtained and used in violation of basic ethical precepts and statutory obligations.

Unlike most disqualification situations where the knowledge eventually requiring disqualification is acquired innocently by the attorney in the course of affording a client representation, here the knowledge has been obtained by improper design and the use of the information is not merely a prospect to be avoided by prophylactic disqualification, but an accomplished fact. In these respects the abuse with which we are presently concerned is far more serious than that which is ordinarily addressed or sought to be averted where disqualification is ordered. (*Cf. Greene v. Greene*, 47 NY 2d 447, 453.)

It is, of course, regrettable that the action we now find it necessary to take will deprive petitioner of his chosen counsel. This is, however, unavoidable given the gravity of the conduct involved and its highly prejudicial consequences for the Trustee. Confronted as we are with a course of activity exhibiting a complete and deliberate disregard for the process by which discovery is to be conducted and a total insensitivity to the strict ethical and legal limitations placed upon the disclosure and use of privileged material, to impose a sanction short of disqualification would be to treat the conduct at issue with a degree of lenity practically inviting its recurrence. Our principal concern under the circumstances must be to preserve the integrity of the process by which rights are vindicated."

19. "Whether or not it can be said that the Trustee's attorney-client privilege has been compromised, and it would appear that it has at least with regard to those consultations the Trustee had with Greenbaum on behalf of the family businesses, it is clear beyond doubt that she has been prejudiced by the unauthorized disclosure to petitioner of material not otherwise obtainable. Much of the material contains evidence of communications between the Trustee and the Greenbaum firm in confidence, the release of which is at a minimum

embarrassing to the Trustee and, more importantly, is damaging to her prospects in the current litigation. That this disclosure could have been prevented by the Trustee had her opportunity to do so not been subverted by petitioner's counsel is now decidedly plain. In view of the fact that the documents involved were not otherwise obtainable, the very deprivation by petitioner's counsel of the Trustee's opportunity to contest the disclosure before the fact constitutes substantial prejudice under CPLR 3103(c). Having made this observation, it is important to reiterate that although the case for suppression is made compelling by the fact that the matter disclosed was privileged and, therefore, not otherwise obtainable, suppression on the terms imposed by the Surrogate would have been warranted in this case even if the material were otherwise unobtainable. It is not only the unauthorized disclosure of the documents from the Greenbaum files that has prejudiced the Trustee, but as noted, their actual use in the present litigation."

20. Unreported (EDNY, September 2, 1988).

21. See National Law Journal (April 25, 1988) at 16.

22. Note Remine and Gilbert, "Discovery: Abuses, Sanctions and Ethical Concerns," Trial Magazine (January 1987) at 53 et seq.

23. 96 S Ct 2778 (1976).

24. Unreported (Ariz., July 17, 1986).

25. See Trial Magazine (August 1987) at 51.

26. Note Smith v. Superior Court, 198 Cal Rptr 829 (1984) at 834.

27. 113 Cal Rptr 296 (1974).

28. 77 Mo 64 (1882) at 86.

29. 384 F Supp 821 (WD Ark., 1974).

30. 424 So2d 596 (Ala., 1982).

31. See Public Health Trust of Dade County v. Valcin, 5097 So2d 596 (Fla., 1987).

32. Supra note 25 at 53.

33. Supra note 22 at 56. See also Friends of All Children, Inc. v. Lockheed Aircraft Corp., 587 F Supp 180 (DC., 1984).

34. 593 F Supp 1443 (CD Cal., 1984).

35. Note Gage, "Alteration, Falsification and Fabrication of Records in Malpractice Action," 1981 Med Trial Tech Q 476 (1981).

36. Unreported (SDNY, November 3, 1988).

37. Pub L 89-554, 80 Stat 383 (1966), codified at 5 USC 552 (1987).

38. See generally 11 Environ Aff 805 (1984) at 814 et seq.

39. See Warren Freedman, Federal Statutes on Environmental Protection (1987).

40. See EPA v. Mink, 410 US 73 (1973) at 80.

41. Supra note 22 at 63.

42. 441 US 281 (1979).

43. See 47 Fed Reg 14874 (1982).

44. See Note, "The Freedom of Information Act—A Potential Alternative to Conventional Criminal Discovery," 14 Am Crim L Rev 73 (1976).

45. 5 USC 552a (1976).

46. "[A]nd the activities of prosecutors, courts, correctional, probation, pardon, or parole authorities, and which consists of (A) information compiled for the purpose of identifying individual criminal offenders and alleged offenders and consisting only of identifying data and notations of arrests, the nature and disposition of criminal charges, sentencing, confinement, release and parole and probation status; (B) information compiled for the purpose of a criminal investigation, including reports of informants and investigators, and associated with an indentifiable individual; or (C) reports identifiable to an individual compiled at any state of the process of enforcement of the criminal laws from arrest or indictment through release from supervision." (5 USC § 552(c)(j)(2).)

47. New York Public Officers Law §§ 84 et seq.

48. See generally Trial Magazine (December 1987) at 23 et seq., and For the Defense (June 1987) at 25 et seq.

49. 526 F2d 28 (Alaska, 1974).

50. See Henke v. Iowa Home Mutual Casualty Co., 87 NW2d 290 (Iowa, 1958).

51. 452 So2d 861 (Ala., 1984).

52. 670 P2d 725 (Ariz., 1983).

53. See Hartford Accident and Indemnity Co. v. Chung and Midland-Ross Corp. v. Swartz, 176 NW2d 735 (Nebr., 1979).

54. Defense Counsel J. (January 1988) at 51.

55. Id. at 59.

56. "The signature of an attorney or party constitutes a certificate by him that he has read the pleading, motion, or other paper; that to the best of his knowledge, information, and belief formed after reasonable inquiry is well grounded in fact and is warranted by existing law or a good faith argument for the extension, modification, or reversal of existing law, and that it is not interposed for improper purpose, such as to harass or to cause unnecessary delay or needless increase in the cost of litigation. . . . If a pleading, motion, or other paper is signed in violation of this rule, the court, upon motion or upon its own initiative, shall impose upon the person who signed it, a represented party, or both, an appropriate sanction, which may include an order to pay to the other party or parties the amount of the reasonable expenses incurred because of the filing of the pleading, motion, or other paper, including a reasonable attorney's fee."

57. See Brown v. National Board of Medical Examiners, 800 F2d 168 (7th Cir., 1986).

58. 634 F Supp 72 (SD Miss., 1986).

59. See Freedman, Frivolous Lawsuits.

60. Supra note 54 at 53–54.

61. Unreported (Del., August 9, 1984).

62. Id.

63. 88 Cal Rptr 337 (1970).

64. Unreported (NY County, May 3, 1988).

65. Rule 11, as amended in 1983, provides: *"Signings of Pleadings, Motions, and Other Papers—Sanctions.* Every pleading, motion, and other paper of a party represented by an attorney shall be signed by at least one attorney of record in his individual name, whose address shall be stated. A party who is not represented by an attorney shall sign his pleading, motion, or other paper and state his address. Except then otherwise specifically provided by rule or statute, pleadings need not be verified or accompanied by affidavit. The rule in equity that the averments of an answer under oath must be overcome by the testimony of two witnesses or of one witness sustained by corroborating circumstances is abolished. The signature of an attorney or party constitutes a certificate by him that he has read the pleading, motion, or other paper; that to the best of his knowledge, information, and belief formed after reasonable inquiry it is well-grounded in fact and is warranted by existing law or a good faith argument for the extension, modification, or reversal of existing law, and that it is not interposed for any improper purpose, such as to harass or to cause unnecessary delay or needless increase in the cost of litigation. If a pleading, motion, or other paper is not signed, it shall be stricken unless it is signed promptly after the omission is called to the attention of the pleader or movant. If a pleading, motion, or other paper is signed in violation of this rule, the court, upon motion or upon its own initiative, shall impose upon the person who signed it, a represented party, or both, an appropriate sanction, which may include an order to pay to the other party or parties the amount of the reasonable expenses incurred because of the filing of the pleading, motion, or other paper, including a reasonable attorney's fee."

66. Rule 37 provides in pertinent part: *"Failure to Make or Cooperate in Discovery—Sanctions.*

(b) Failure to Comply with Order.

(1) Sanctions by Court in District Where Deposition is Taken. If a deponent fails to be sworn or to answer a question after being directed to do so by the court in the district in which the deposition is being taken, the failure may be considered a contempt of that court.

(2) Sanctions by Court in Which Action is Pending. If a party or an officer, director, or managing agent of a party or a person designated under Rule 30(b)(6) or 31(a) to testify on behalf of a party fails to obey an order to provide or permit discovery, including an order made under subdivision (a) of this rule or Rule 35, or if a party fails to obey an order entered under Rule 26(f), the court in which the action is pending may make such orders in regard to the failure as are just, and among others the following:

(A) An order that the matters regarding which the order was made or any other designated facts shall be taken to be established for the purposes of the action in accordance with the claim of the party obtaining the order;

(B) An order refusing to allow the disobedient party to support or choose designated claims or defenses, or prohibiting him from introducing designated matters in evidence;

(C) An order striking out pleadings or parts thereof, or staying further proceedings until the order is obeyed, or dismissing the action or proceeding or any part thereof, or rendering a judgement by default against the disobedient party;

(D) In lieu of any of the foregoing orders or in addition thereto, an order treating as a contempt of court the failure to obey any orders except an order to submit to a physical or mental examination.

(E) Where a party has failed to comply with an order under Rule 35(a) requiring him to produce another for examination, such orders as are listed in paragraphs (A), (B), and (C) of this subdivision, unless the party failing to comply shows that he is unable to produce such person for examination.

In lieu of any of the foregoing orders or in addition thereto, the court shall require the party failing to obey the order or the attorney advising him or both to pay the reasonable expenses, including attorney's fees, caused by the failure, unless the court finds that the failure was substantially justified or that other circumstances make an award of expenses unjust.''

67. See Damiani v. Rhode Island Hospital, 704 F2d 12 (1st Cir., 1983).

68. See Lorin v. Goto & Co., 700 F2d 1202 (8th Cir., 1983).

69. Note Minnesota Mining & Manufacturing Co. v. ECO Chemicals, Inc., 757 F2d 1256 (7th Cir., 1985).

70. See Shearson Loeb Rhoades, Inc. v. Quinard, 751 F2d 1102 (9th Cir., 1985).

71. Id.

72. See Van Nostrand v. University of Minnesota, 656 F2d 315 (8th Cir., 1981).

73. Unreported (2d Cir. March 14, 1988), aff'g 635 F Supp 228 (SDNY, 1987).

74. See New York Law Journal (March 24, 1988) at 1.

75. 102 FRD 472 (SDFla, 1984).

76. Id. at 476.

77. Id. at 478.

78. Id. at 479. See generally Trial Magazine (February 1987) at 69.

79. Id. at 483.

80. 775 F2d 1440 (11th Cir., 1985).

81. Unreported (SDNY, 1987).

82. 514 NYS2d 756 (2nd Dept., 1987).

83. "Although Coca-Cola's director of engineering, who permitted the machine to be scrapped, stated that he was unaware of the course of the litigation, it is undisputed that he was previously contacted with regard to arranging an inspection of the machine. Furthermore, Coca-Cola was under a duty to inform the director of engineering with respect to the court's order directing the inspection of the machine, especially since A-B-C had consistently made its desire to inspect the machine (which was at the center of the instant litigation) known. Under these circumstances, Coca-Cola has not offered a reasonable explanation for its disposal of the machine. . . ."

84. Unreported (2d Cir., May 2, 1988).

85. See generally Trial Magazine (February 1987) at 70.

86. FED. R. CRIM. P. 16(d)(2) provides in pertinent part: "(2) Failure to Comply With a Request. If at any time during the course of the proceedings it is brought to the attention of the court that a party has failed to comply with this rule, the court may order such party to permit the discovery or inspection, grant a continuance, or prohibit the party from introducing evidence not disclosed, or it may enter such other order as it deems just under the circumstances. The court may specify the time, place and manner of making the discovery and inspection and may prescribe such terms and conditions as are just."

87. 508 F2d 1001 (7th Cir, 1975).

88. See United States v. Lambert, 580 F2d 740 (5th Cir., 1978) where the court utilized the remedy of a continuance so as to allow an inspection of the discovery material.

89. See Joseph, "Rule 11 is Only the Beginning," A.B.A.J. (May 1, 1988) at 62 et seq.

90. Note United Energy Owners Committee, Inc. v. U.S. Energy Managers Systems, Inc., 837 F2d 356 (9th Cir., 1988).

91. See Joseph, "The Law of Sanctions," Trial Magazine (May 1988) at 40 et seq.

92. Note Thomas v. Capital Securities Service, Inc., 836 F2d 866 (5th Cir., 1988).

93. See Chevron, USA, Inc. v. Hand, 763 F2d 1184 (10th Cir., 1985).

94. See Adduono v. World Hockey Assn., 824 F2d 617 (8th Cir., 1987).

95. Supra note 91 at 59.

96. See Murphy v. Magnolia Electric Power Assn., 639 F2d 232 (5th Cir., 1981).

97. Supra note 89 at 65.

98. See State of Wisconsin v. Glick, 782 F2d 670 (7th Cir., 1986).

99. Unreported (2d Cir., 1987).

100. 502 So2d 523 (Fla. App., 1987).

101. 518 NYS2d 622 (1st Dept., 1987).

102. Unreported (Conn. Super., 1987).

103. See Maute, ''Sporting Theory of Justice: Taming Adversary Zeal with a Logical Sanctions Doctrine,'' 20 Conn L Rev 7 (1987).

104. See Chapter 11.

105. Supra note 103 at 66.

106. See Abney, ''Spoliation and Future Civil Actions: Slowing the Rush to a Novel Tort,'' National Law Journal (February 2, 1987) at 38.

107. See 1 Adelaide L Rev (Australia) 344 (1962).

108. (1961) Law Soc Judg, Scheme 11.

109. Supra note 107.

110. ''A good illustration of the application of this principle can be seen in the famous case of *Armory v. Delamirie* (1844, 8 Jur. 964). Since the jeweller failed to produce the jewel found by the chimney sweep, the court adopted the presumption that it was of the highest quality and assessed damages accordingly. In applying this principle, as the court in *Saloustis v. Nikic* hastened to point out, one must distinguish between a case of intentional suppression of vital evidence, and one where secondary evidence is given and the unknown parts cannot reasonably be thought to have any effect upon the issue.

The second obstacle the plaintiff had to face in seeking rescission in equity was the maxim that he who seeks equity must do equity, or alternatively, the principle that the plaintiff 'must come into the court with propriety of conduct, with ''clean hands.'' ' The principle, as Mayo J. well recognised, must 'have an immediate and necessary relation to the equity sued for' (*Dering v. Earl of Minchelsea* [1878] 1 Cox Eq. 318, 319–320). The plaintiff's own wrongful act had a direct bearing on the claim, and this principle was rightly applied.

There seems to be little difference in effect between the principle of evidence and that of equity applied by the Court. The earliest authority for the application of the former is to be found in 1680, in the court of Chancery, when Lord Nottingham L.C. said in *Lewis v. Lewis* ([1680] Cas. temp. Finch 471; 23 E.R. 254 at 255): 'where the evidence is suppressed by either party, a court of equity will always presume a title against the person suppressing it, until the evidence be produced.' From here it has become a rule of evidence in courts of common law and equity (See Cookes v. Hellier [1749] 1 Ves. Sen. 234, 235), and it may be doubted whether it has any wider application than the principle that a plaintiff must come to equity with clean hands.''

111. 151 Cal App3d 491, 198 Cal Rptr 829 (1984).

112. ''The seventh cause of action specifically alleged that after the accident, Abbott Ford promised the Smiths' counsel that it 'would maintain securely in their care, possession, custody and control for later examination and testing by Plaintiffs' technical experts the left rear tire and wheel, lug bolts, lug nuts and brake drum which these Defendants [Abbott Ford] had removed from Defendant['s] van.'

It was further alleged that Abbott Ford knew that such physical evidence would be essential proof in a civil action to be brought by the Smiths, and that Abbott Ford knew or should have known that the Smiths would be induced to rely upon its promise by forebearing from seeking a temporary restraining order to compel it to maintain the evidence securely.

These allegations were incorporated by reference into the eighth cause of action, which specifically stated that Abbott Ford 'willfully, wrongfully, and intentionally, and with conscious disregard of the probable serious harm to Plaintiffs, and with malice and reckless indifference for the injurious consequences of their acts, conceded, lost, destroyed or otherwise disposed of the physical evidence which they had promised to maintain for Plaintiffs.'

The damage alleged was the 'significant prejudice' of the Smiths' opportunity to obtain compensation for their grievous physical and emotional injuries.

Abbott Ford demurred to the seventh and eighth causes of action on the grounds they failed to state a cause of action.''

113. Id. at 493 and 831, respectively.

114. ''[T] he progress of the common law is marked by many cases of first impression, in which the court has struck out boldly to create a new cause of action, where none had been recognized before. The intentional infliction of mental suffering . . . the invasion of [the] right of privacy, the denial of [the] right to vote, the conveyance of land to defeat a title, the infliction of prenatal injuries, the alienation of the affections of a parent . . . to name only a few instances, could not be fitted into any accepted classifications when they first arose, but nevertheless have been held to be torts. The law of torts is anything but static, and the limits of its development are never set. *When it becomes clear that the plaintiff's interests are entitled to legal protection against the conduct of the defendant,* the mere fact that the claim is novel will not of itself operate as a bar to a remedy'' [emphasis added; Prosser, Torts, (4th ed. 1971) § 1, pp. 3–4). ''The common thread woven into all torts is the idea of *unreasonable interference with the interests of others*'' [emphasis added; *id.*, at p.6].

''California has long recognized '[f]or every wrong there is a remedy.' (Civ. Code. § 3523), and has allowed for new torts through the legislative and judicial process. (4 Witkin, Summary of Cal.Law [8th ed. 1974] Torts § 10, p. 2310.) Legal protection has been afforded recently in the area of wrongful birth (*Stills v. Gratton* [1976] 55 Cal.App.3d 698, 127 Cal.Rptr. 652) and wrongful life (*Turpin v. Sortini* (1982)31 Cal.3d 220, 182 Cal.Rptr. 337, 643 P.2d 954).

In light of the foregoing, we believe that a new tort may be appropriate to cover the intentional spoliation of evidence, since it meets the criteria spelled out by Prosser and recognized by case law.''

115. See Warren Freedman, Res Judicata and Collateral Estoppel (1988).

116. Penal Code section 135 states: ''Every person who, knowing that any book, paper, record, instrument in writing, or other matter or thing, is about

to be produced in evidence upon any trial, inquiry, or investigation whatever, authorized by law, willfully destroys or conceals the same, with intent thereby to prevent it from being produced, is guilty of a misdemeanor.'' According to the court, ''*Agnew v. Parks* (1959) 172 Cal.App.2d 756, 766, 343 P.2d 118, interpreted the crime set forth in section 135 as an 'obstruction of justice' for which only the state can prosecute, and held that there is no civil cause of action available to the party harmed.''

117. The court reasoned that ''the most troubling aspect in allowing a cause for intentional spoliation of evidence is the requisite tort element of damages proximately resulting from defendant's alleged act. Here, the underlying product liability case has not yet gone to trial and it is possible that the Smiths could prove their case through other means and recover damages. We appreciate that one who has suffered a legally recognized injury is usually entitled to an award of damages. (Dobbs, Remedies, Damages-Equity-Restitution (1973) § 3.1, p. 135.) However, a plaintiff must not only establish the fact of damages with reasonable certainty, but must also prove the amount of damages with reasonable certainty. (*Id.*, at § 3.3, p.150.)

The United States Supreme Court provides some guidance in this difficult area. Over 50 years ago it held that '[w] here the *tort itself* is of such a nature as to preclude the ascertainment of the amount of damages with certainty, it would be a perversion of fundamental principles of justice to deny all relief to the injured person, and thereby relieve the wrongdoer from making any amend for his acts. In such case, while the damages may not be determined by mere speculation or guess, it will be enough if the evidence show the extent of the damages as a matter of just and reasonable inference, although the result be only approximate.' (emphasis added; *Story Parchment Co. v. Paterson P. Paper Co.* (1931) 282 U.S. 555, 563, 51 S.Ct. 248, 250, 75 L.Ed. 544, 548 (action for damages arising under Sherman Antitrust Act for alleged conspiracy); see e.g. *Turpin v. Sortini, supra,* 31 Cal.3d at p. 235, 182 Cal.Rptr. 337, 643 p.2d 954.)

Courts since then have taken the position that plaintiffs are expected to prove damages with as much accuracy as reasonably possible but 'precision not attainable in the nature of the claim and circumstances is not ordinarily required.' ''

118. ''This tort permits recovery for interference with business relationships or *expectations* even in the absence of a legally binding agreement or where the *expectations* of the parties are only the subject of an unenforceable contract. (*Buckaloo v. Johnson* (1975) 14 Cal.3d 815, 822–823, 122 Cal.Rptr. 745, 537 P.2d 865; *Lowell v. Mother's Cake & Cookie Co.* (1978) 79 Cal.App.3d 13, 17, 144 Cal.Rptr. 664.) . . . While it is admitted that the test for intentional interference with prospective business advantage is sometimes vague, it is now widely recognized and has rapidly developed since Supreme Court recognition in *Buckaloo.* (*Lowell v. Mother's Cake & Cookie*

Co . . . supra, 79 Cal.App.3d at pp. 17–18, 144 Cal.Rptr. 664; 4 Witkin, Summary of Cal.Law, *op. cit. supra,* § 392, p. 2643.)

Prosser in discussing this particular tort, observed that 'a large part of what is most valuable in modern life depends upon "probable expectancies," [and] as social and industrial life become more complex the courts must do more to discover, define and protect them from undue interference.' (Prosser, Torts, *supra,* § 130, p. 950; *Worldwide Commerce, Inc. v. Fruehauf Corp.* (1978) 84 Cal.App.3d 803, 811, 149 Cal.Rptr. 42.)

California courts have adopted Prosser's belief in the importance of 'probable expectancies' in several cases dealing with interference with prospective business advantage, requiring only an allegation of a 'reasonable probability' that a contract or profit would have been obtained but for the defendant's acts. (*Campbell v. Rayburn* (1954) 129 Cal.App.2d 232, 235, 276 P.2d 671; *Brody v. Montalbano* (1978) 87 Cal.App.3d 725, 738, 151 Cal.Rptr. 206; see also *Gold v. Los Angeles Democratic League* (1975) 49 Cal.App.3d 365, 375, 122 Cal.Rptr. 732.)"

119. Supra note 105.

120. 34 Cal3d 18, 192 Cal Rptr. 233, 664 P2d 137 (1983).

121. Supra note 111.

122. According to the court, "As a rule, one has no duty to come to the aid of another. A person who has not created a peril is not liable in tort merely for failure to take affirmative action to assist or protect another unless there is some relationship between them which gives rise to a duty to act. (Rest.2d Torts, § 314; 4 Witkin, Summary of Cal. Law (8th ed.) Torts, § 554, p. 2821.) (3) Also pertinent to our discussion is the role of the volunteer who, having no initial duty to do so, undertakes to come to the aid of another—the 'good Samaritan.' He is under a duty to exercise due care in performance and is liable if (a) his failure to exercise such care increases the risk of such harm, or (b) the harm is suffered because of the other's reliance upon the undertaking. (Rest.2d Torts, § 323.)

Application of these general principles in the area of law enforcement and other police activities has produced some confusion and conflict. To an extent, the concepts are muddied by widely held misconceptions concerning the duty owed by police to individual members of the general public. . . .

In spite of the fact that our tax dollars support police functions, it is settled that the rules concerning the duty—or lack thereof—to come to the aid of another area applicable to law enforcement personnel in carrying out routine traffic investigations. Thus, the state highway patrol has the right but not the duty, to investigate accidents. . . . Nevertheless, although 'no special relationship may exist between members of the California Highway Patrol and the motoring public generally, or between the Patrol and stranded motorists generally' . . . when the state, through its agents, voluntarily assumes a protective duty toward a certain member of the public and undertakes action on behalf of that member, thereby inducing reliance, it is held to the same standard of care as a private person or organization. . . .

The breach of duty may be an affirmative act which places the person in peril or increases the risk of harm as in *McCorkle v. Los Angeles* (1969) 70 Cal. 2d 252 [74 Cal.Rptr. 389, 449 P.2d 453], where an officer investigating an accident directed the plaintiff to follow him into the middle of the intersection where the plaintiff was hit by another car. The negligence may also constitute an omission or failure to act, as in *Morgan v. County of Yuba* (1964) 230 Cal.App.2d 938 [41 CalRptr.508], where a deputy sheriff promised to warn a decedent if a prisoner, who had made threats on her life, was released. The county was held liable when the sheriff failed to warn.

This does not mean that a promise and reliance thereon are indispensable elements of a special relationship. Such a relationship has also been found when the *conduct* of a police officer, in a situation of dependency, results in detrimental reliance on him for protection. A special relationship based on such dependency was found in *Mann v. State of California, supra,* 70 Cal.App.3d 773. Highway patrolmen, coming to the aid of a stranded motorist, placed their car with flashing lights behind two cars stalled on the freeway. After calling the tow truck, the officers withdrew without warning; they did not wait for the tow truck to line up behind the stalled car or provide the alternative protection of flares. Minutes later the stalled car was sideswiped by a passing car and the persons nearby were injured. In *Mann,* the officers' conduct contributed to, increased, and changed the risk which would have otherwise existed. They stopped to investigate and they took affirmative steps to provide assistance, lulling the injured parties into a false sense of security and perhaps preventing other assistance from being sought."

123. See Velasco v. Commercial Building Maintenance Co., 161 Cal App3d 874, 215 Cal Rptr 504 (1985).

124. Supra note 106.

125. 473 So2d 1307 (Fla. App., 1984).

126. See generally 20 U of Richmond L Rev 191 (1985).

127. Cf. Spano v. McAvoy, 589 F Supp 423 (NDNY, 1984), holding that routine destruction of departmental tape recordings precluded a finding of intentional spoliation. Also cf. Reid v. State Farm Mutual Auto Insurance Co., 218 Cal Rptr 913 (2d Dist., 1985) to the effect that the insurer had no special relationship with the permissive user of the insured automobile requiring the insurer to preserve a worthless auto as evidence for a remotely possible lawsuit.

128. 718 P2d 456 (Alaska, 1986).

129. According to 69 Minn L Rev 961 (1985) at 962: "A court asked to recognize the new tort of intentional spoliation of evidence must first determine whether the right to bring a personal injury lawsuit is a legally protectable interest. If the court determines that the interest is deserving of legal

protection, it must next decide whether interference with that interest by intentional spoliation of evidence is tortious conduct. In doing so, the court must determine how to apply the traditional tort elements of intent, causation, and damages. In addition, because most states, like California, have a criminal statute that proscribes the intentional destruction of evidence, the court must consider whether the existence of criminal sanctions precludes the plaintiff's tort action. Finally, in determining whether to recognize a separate tort action, the court must measure the adequacy of existing means of dealing with spoliation of evidence within the framework of the underlying litigation itself.''

130. Cf. Agnew v. Parks, 172 Cal App2d 756, 343 P2d 118 (1959).

131. Supra note 129.

132. Id. at 973 to 976.

133. See Fox v. Cohen, 406 NE2d 178 (Ill. Appl., 1980).

134. Supra note 123.

135. See INA Aviation Corp. v. United States, 468 F Supp 695 (EDNY, 1979), aff 610 F2d 806 (2d Cir., 1979).

136. 507 A2d 1046 (DC, 1986).

137. See generally 36 Catholic U L Rev 761 (1987).

138. 427 US 639 (1976).

139. ``[T]his action was taken in the face of warnings that their failure . . . could result in the imposition of sanctions under Fed. R. Civ. P. 37. If the sanction of dismissal is not warranted by the circumstances of this case, then the court can envisage no set of facts whereby that sanction should ever be applied.''

140. Note DC Super, Ct Civ R 37(b): ``Failure to Comply with Order. . . .

(2) Sanctions by this Court. If a party . . . fails to obey an order to provide or permit discovery, . . . the Court may make such orders in regard to the failure as are just, and among others the following:

(A) An order that the matters regarding which the order was made or any other designated facts shall be taken to be established . . . ;

(B) An order refusing to allow the disobedient party to support or oppose designated claims or offenses, or prohibiting him from introducing designated matters in evidence;

(C) An order striking out pleadings or parts thereof, or staying further proceedings until the order is obeyed, or dismissing the action or proceedings until the order is obeyed, or dismissing the action or proceeding or any part thereof, or rendering a judgment by default against the disobedient party;

(D) In lieu of any of the foregoing orders or in addition thereto, an order treating as a Contempt of Court the failure to obey any orders except an order to submit to a physical or mental examination.''

141. The fact pattern of the Hinkle case is as follows: ``The action commenced in June 1983, when the plaintiff filed an action to recover for a breach

of contract by defendants Hinkle and Johnson. The defendants' counsel filed a timely answer and counterclaims. On July 5, 1983, the plaintiff began discovery by serving the defendants with interrogatories and notices of deposition. When the defendants ignored these requests, the plaintiff repeated them in October 1983. Still, the defendants completely failed to answer or object to the interrogatories, and failed to appear for their depositions. In November 1983, five months after commencing the action, and four months after initiating discovery, the plaintiff filed a motion to compel discovery by the defendants. The defendants were served with copies of this motion and were given notice of the hearing. Both Hinkle and Johnson continued to completely ignore the case and neither of them replied to the motion, attended or sent representation to the hearing. Judge Henry Greene granted the motion to compel discovery on January 11, 1984. The order compelling discovery set deadlines for Hinkle and Johnson to answer the interrogatories and to submit to depositions. He also entered a default judgment against them contingent upon their further unexcused refusal to comply with discovery rules. Because the trial date was only two weeks away, the judge granted the plaintiff's request to postpone trial. Both deadlines passed without the defendants either answering the interrogatories or giving depositions. The plaintiff moved for a default judgment under the terms of the order. Superior Court Judge Murphy granted the motion after an adversary hearing, and the defendants appealed.

In *Hinkle,* the District of Columbia Court of Appeals confronted a flagrant abuse of discovery. There had been a complete frustration of the discovery process by parties who flagrantly ignored the court's orders. The court found that severe circumstances existed, and that the defendants' knowing failure to comply with the orders satisfied the willfulness factor. The opinion concluded that prejudice to the party seeking discovery existed due to the plaintiff's lost opportunity for a judgment and the frustration of waiting for answers from the defendants. The court of appeals affirmed the dismissal, finding no abuse of discretion. The *Hinkle* court thus signaled that delay as prejudice can be established when the delay results from disregard of discovery norms.'' Supra note 114 at 771–772.

142. Prosser, Handbook of the Law of Torts (4th ed., 1971) at 6.

143. Supra note 129 at 972.

144. Supra note 126 at 110.

145. See generally 6 ALR4th 195 (1981) at 201. Note Bigelow v. RKO Radio Pictures, 327 US 251 (1946) where the highest court had occasion to comment: ''where the defendant by his own wrong has prevented a more precise computation, the jury may not render a verdict based on speculation or guesswork. But the jury may make a just and reasonable estimate of the damage based on relevant data, and render its verdict accordingly. . . . Any other rule would enable the wrongdoer to profit by his wrongdoing at the expense of his victim. It would be an inducement to make wrongdoing so

effective and complete in every case as to preclude any recovery, by rendering the measure of damages uncertain. Failure to apply it would mean the more grievous the wrong done, the less likelihood there would be of a recovery. The most elementary conceptions of justice and public policy require the wrongdoer shall bear the risk of the uncertainty which his own wrong has created."

146. Supra note 126 at 114. Also note 45 Yale L J 226 (1936) and 4 Cal Law 15 (June 1984).

147. Unreported (1988).

148. See National Law Journal (February 8, 1988) at 5.

Table of Cases

Index

About the Author

WARREN FREEDMAN was formerly Counsel and Assistant Secretary for Bristol-Myers Co. His previous books include *Foreign Plaintiffs in Products Liability Actions, Frivolous Lawsuits and Frivolous Defenses, Federal Statutes on Environmental Protection, The Right of Privacy in the Computer Age,* and *Professional Sports and Antitrust.*

www.ingramcontent.com/pod-product-compliance
Ingram Content Group UK Ltd.
Pitfield, Milton Keynes, MK11 3LW, UK
UKHW020207290926
15470UKWH00001B/49

9 780899 303321